SHANGHAI

LOVED AND LOST

SHANGHAI

LOVED AND LOST

ELIZABETH SHAEN

Published by
Ajijic Books Publishing

Cover and book design: Mike Riley, www.ajijicbooks.com
Publisher: Ajijic Books Publishing, Chapala, Mexico
and Ottawa, Canada.

In loving memory of my late husband, Duncan.
Sadly, he died before this book was finished.

ACKNOWLEDGEMENTS

My sincerest thanks go to all my wonderful friends and family who never failed in their encouragement and enthusiasm for this book. My special thanks go to Ian Colterjohn, Duncan's cousin. Ian and his sister, Maureen, are the only surviving family members who lived through the years of this story and were part of it. I must also thank Michael Kolterjahn (in Sweden) and Tom Kolterjahn (in the USA) most sincerely for sharing their genealogical and family research with me. I could not have written the Colterjahn/Colterjohn history in the prologue without their help.

I am lost for words to express my enormous gratitude to my wonderful editor, Bonnie Baker-Cowan. She took my ignorance and somehow managed to mold it into something that we are both proud of. The same can be said for Mike Riley, my book designer, whose professionalism has made it a pleasure to work with him. Lastly, but not least, my sincerest thanks go to Antoinette Bullock for the illustration on the cover. She expressed my thoughts perfectly.

AUTHOR'S NOTE

This is the story of my late husband's family and is, to the best of my knowledge, true in all the facts. Occasionally, I have used my creative skills to give the book a little more color, but this has never changed the truth of events or the actions and personalities of the people concerned. It covers one hundred years, starting with the arrival of Wilhelm Colterjahn in Scotland from Germany in 1855, and progresses through two World Wars and three continents to finish in Scotland again in 1955. However, the main focus of the tale is in Shanghai, China. Duncan, my husband, always wanted me to write this story so I have made him the narrator. It is his voice that I heard in my head as I was writing.

I was lucky to have original material to work with, including photos and scrapbooks with newspaper cuttings from old Shanghai papers. I met the family in 1951, only two years after they finally returned from China for good, and knew them well. Those years in Shanghai were part of everyday conversations for the rest of their lives, and my parents-in-law's house was filled with beautiful Chinese rugs and artifacts, many of which I am now proud to own. In the last five years of my husband's life, he dictated his memoirs onto tapes, and these have provided a rich resource.

Concurrent with the family saga, are a hundred years of Chinese history and politics. This spans the fascinating era from the first opium war in 1842, which resulted in the creation of five treaty ports and the opening up of international trade with China, to the takeover by the Communists in 1949. My research for this led me to many really exceptional books. My favorites are listed in the bibliography at the end of this book, and I thank the authors with all my heart for helping me to understand the China of those days. I found that, while the basic facts and dates remained more or less consistent, the portrayal and interpretation of these events sometimes varied widely, so I resorted to dozens of hours of research on the Internet in search of anything relevant to my subject. This helped me to walk a careful path through this historical jungle and to draw my own conclusions. I am sure many readers will question my version, but it was written with an honest attempt to record events without bias.

Elizabeth Shaen Colterjohn
November 2014

NOMENCLATURE OF CHINESE NAMES

I have chosen to use the names of Chinese places and rivers that were commonly used by the foreign community in Shanghai at the time that this story took place. Even then, there were often alternative ways of spelling those names. Today, most of these have completely different names, so I have listed some of the places that have featured most in this book, to help the reader identify them. The modern names are on the right.

	LATIN (Romantic)	PINYIN (modern)
Rivers:	Soochow	Suzhou
	Whangpoo / Whangpu	Huangpu
	Yellow River	Huang He
Cities:	Canton	Guangzhou
	Chapei	Zhabei
	Chungking	Chongqing
	Foochow	Fuzhou
	Honk Kong	Xianggang
	Lunghwa	Longhua
	Mukden	Shenyang
	Nanking	Nanjing
	Peking	Beijing
	Pootung	Pudong
	Szechuan	Sichuan
	Suchow	Xuzhou
	Tientsin	Jinan
	Tsingtao	Quingdao
Islands:	Formosa	Taiwan
	Pescadores	Penghu

Contents

x

PROLOGUE: SCOTLAND

1700 - 1926

The 18th century laid the foundations for modern Scotland. It started with the Acts of Union in 1706 and 1707, which created the United Kingdom of Great Britain. Although it had taken the Scots a lot of persuading that it was to their advantage, once it was law, they exploited the new opportunities it provided with enthusiasm, especially with regard to trade. The demand for new and faster ships gave an economic boost to ship-building in both Glasgow and Leith, and in 1720 Leith built the first dry dock in Scotland. Within ten years, Glasgow's ships had joined the English tobacco trade with America, and by 1758 Scottish tobacco imports were greater than in all the English ports combined.

Education has always been of utmost importance to Scots of all classes, as a love of learning is instilled in their souls. The seeds of the Scottish Enlightenment were sown early in the 18th century by a Presbyterian minister seeking the meaning of life. This was taken up by university professors in Glasgow and Edinburgh, who broke precedent by changing their lectures from Latin to English, and the new philosophies quickly spilled over into the taverns and tea-houses. Unlike the French enlightenment, this became a middle-class movement and working men could be found arguing in the public houses as to whether a man was born sinful and had to learn to be good, or whether the reverse was true. All this taught Scotsmen to think and argue the validity of their ideas. Literature on all subjects increased substantially, initiated by Adam Smith and Lord Kames, and expanded by many other famous men through the years like Robbie Burns and Sir Walter Scott. By the mid-1700s, the Lowlands were experiencing a surge of economic and cultural growth.

Scots, or North Britons as they were now called, gradually filtered south and found that their superior education stood them in good stead. They were not always the ones to invent new concepts but they inevitably developed practical applications for them. Scots soon found themselves assimilating into London society and leading the way in new projects and ideas. This, in turn, created a wave of *Anglicization* in Lowland Scotland, with the upper and middle classes learning to speak English, rather than Scots, and adopting more *polite* ways. The English soon followed by coming north and buying land in Scotland for fishing and shooting. Englishmen and Scotsmen were finally learning to work and play together.

However, things in the Highlands deteriorated drastically throughout the 18th century. As early as the mid-1600s, it was recognised that there were too many people in the Highlands for the land to support, yet the population continued to grow. The Jacobite Risings destabilized the way of life, with clans divided in their loyalties. Highlanders began to move to the Lowlands or the coast to find a better way of life. The defeat of Bonny Prince Charlie and the Jacobite army at Culloden in 1745 caused the collapse of the traditional Highland structure; massive land clearances followed. As wealthy Englishmen bought up the most desirable land for recreational estates, whole communities were evicted and their villages razed to make way for sheep and sporting lodges. Those unable to find a living elsewhere, were forced to emigrate. Over the following century, hundreds of thousands of Scots found themselves starting a new life in America, Canada or Australia. Scotland's loss was their gain. Scots were welcomed everywhere; they gave much and demanded little. They were hardy, loyal, honest, hardworking, and better educated than most immigrants, so quickly earned positions of responsibility.

❀ ❀ ❀ ❀ ❀

By the middle of the century, both Glasgow and Edinburgh were experiencing unbearable overcrowding, and tendered for proposals to expand the cities. Edinburgh, in particular, had reached a critical point with a population that had grown to about 50,000 by 1750. The old city was more or less confined to the Castle Rock. The castle stood proudly on the highest point at the west end, and one main street, the High Street, descended eastward to Holyrood Palace, the official residence of the British monarchy in Scotland. The population mostly lived in multi-storey stone tenements that clung to the rock like limpets. These were totally without gas, electricity or plumbing, creating waste removal problems unimaginable today. It was common for residents to throw their slops out of the windows, regardless of unfortunate passersby below. The air was fetid and the buildings were blackened by the smoke of coal fires and oil lamps. Narrow closes and wynds twisted between them, some of them so steep that they became stairways.

In 1766, the city fathers acquired about 100 acres north of the lake that lay below the Castle Rock, and a contract was awarded to James Craig to design a new town there. This was planned to house the professional and merchant classes in spacious, terraced, town-houses, situated on wide streets and crescents often around small parks. There were no provisions for estate lots for large individual homes; these still remained outside the town. Development started soon afterwards, and a causeway was built across the lake to connect the old and the new called The Mound. Strict planning rules were enforced to provide uniformity and harmony to the eye.

Robert Adam and his family of architects received many of the construction contracts and he introduced his new neo-classical style. This had already made him famous in England. The pinnacle of his success was Charlotte Square on the west side of New Town, with its beautiful buildings and perfect symmetry. Although Robert Adam died in 1792, and the project was not completed until about 1820, William Playfair finished the New Town loyal to the original Adam designs. New buildings were also constructed for the University of Edinburgh, the Theatre Royal and several churches. By this time, the population had expanded to over 100,000 and the New Town had burst beyond the confines of the original 100 acres, spreading out in all directions from there. Other architects followed Robert Adam's unique style and Edinburgh became a monument to its own success and a very beautiful city.

⊛   ⊛   ⊛   ⊛   ⊛

During the 50 years between 1815 and 1865, the overseas territory controlled by the British grew by an average of 100,000 square miles per year. This created the Great Diaspora, which would continue almost to the beginning of the Second World War. Unlike the Highland clearances, these men and women were well educated and ambitious, responding to the call of adventure in the ever-expanding British Empire.

Britain had defeated the French in India in 1799, allowing massive expansion there, and later acquired Treaty Ports in China. By 1821, the Hudson Bay Company was administering over 3 million square miles of what would become Canada in 1867. That same year, the British stopped sending convict ships to Australia. Personnel were needed all over the Empire in every capacity, from civil servants for administration to soldiers and sailors to protect the new territories; from tea and cotton farmers in India and Ceylon to rubber planters and tin miners in Malaya; doctors, lawyers, architects and teachers were in big demand; engineers, in particular, were essential to build harbours, bridges and roads all over the world; missionaries went to Africa and China and entrepreneurs found opportunities everywhere. Many of them took their families with them, and they survived incredible hardships with poor pay in those early colonial days, but they kept coming.

The products from all this industry found their way back to Britain to feed the cotton mills and adorn the rich. Fine silks of every hue, ivory and porcelain became the rage in homes of fashion and tea became the polite choice of beverage. Rubber created inflatable tires and golf balls. Britain was at her prime and Queen Victoria was the Empress of it all.

⊛   ⊛   ⊛   ⊛   ⊛

As Britons sailed away to serve Queen and Country, others arrived at her ports from Europe, especially those from the feudal states around the Baltic Sea, looking for freedom and a better way of life. Martin Ferdinand Wilhelm Colterjahn was one of these, and he arrived in Leith some time in 1855. He had been born in 1828, the sixth child of Heinrich Colterjahn and Johanne Graemkow in Mecklenburg-Strelitz, in the northeastern part of Germany. His father was a master shoemaker, burger and toll keeper; a man of property, he was well respected in his community, as were many generations before him. Wilhelm grew up in a large family able to provide their children with some of the finer things in life, including a good basic education, and he apprenticed as a tinsmith.

The defeat of Napoleon at Waterloo in 1815 had finally freed the countries of Europe from tyranny. It was an age of new inventions and the movement of people, but Mecklenburg was not part of these. Divided into two Grand Duchies, it was still ruled by absolute monarchs and permission to marry or leave a duchy still had to be obtained from the Grand Duke. It was not until the eve of the Great War that Mecklenburg-Strelitz received its first constitution. It had always been a poor, agricultural part of Germany, and slipped further behind the rest of the country as the industrial revolution developed.

The younger generation of Colterjahns grew restless, and by 1867 the only child of the eight siblings to be left in Alt Strelitz was Johan Carl Ludwig, an adopted son at the end of the line. Three children had died in infancy or early childhood, three

had emigrated from Germany to America and Wilhelm had
gone to Scotland.

Wilhelm was the first to leave home. With five brothers and
two sisters, he must have felt that his chances of inheriting
much from his father were slim. Like many younger sons, he
chose to seek his fortune by going to sea. The Baltic trading
ships, carrying both goods and passengers, had been sailing
between Germany, the British Isles, Scandinavia and the other
Baltic countries for centuries and were well established and
profitable. This gave him the opportunity to study the many
ports-of-call and plan his future. He probably visited Hamburg
and Leith frequently and chose his future wife in the first and
his new life in the second.

❊   ❊   ❊   ❊   ❊

Leith is situated at the mouth of a river named the *Water of
Leith*, as it flows into the Firth of Forth close to the North Sea.
It was one of the busiest ports in Europe in the 18th and 19th
centuries, and received its share of the cargos arriving from all
over the British Empire. It was a proud and ancient city with
its roots going back to about the 12th century. Not only was it
the seaport for Edinburgh, the capital city of Scotland, but it
had attained the status of an independent burgh in 1833 with
its own town council, and had a history of being the first in
Scotland when it came to civic services. Leith had provided
free schools for boys as early as 1555 and for girls from 1820,
paid for by the trade guilds. Local taxes built and operated free
hospitals from 1777, and an efficient public sewer system was
developed about 1780, although it only flowed into the river.
The first steamship entered the docks in 1813 and by 1821
there was a regular steamship service between London and
Leith three times a week. The Leith Chamber of Commerce
opened its doors in 1840.

Wine and whisky were stored in warehouses from the
1500s, where they were matured and bottled. In fact, this
prompted the building of a number of local glass factories spe-

cialising in the making and exporting of wine bottles. In 1770, the glass industry had expanded and refined the art to include the famous Edinburgh lead crystal, making chandeliers, decanters and cut glass of the highest quality. By the mid-1800s, specialty manufactures included a huge range of products from soap to lead, Rose's Lime Juice to vinegar. Whaling and shipbuilding had always been important to Leith and the *SS Sirius*, one of the first combination steamships to cross the Atlantic, was built there.

However, life in Leith was not only work. There was a golf course and, in 1744, the Honourable Company of Edinburgh Golfers formulated the Rules of Golf which were later adopted by St. Andrew's. They were also one of the first clubs to introduce the new *Gutta-Percha* golf ball after its invention in 1848. Horse races along the beach provided an annual celebration, and soccer and cricket were regular and important events. Horse-drawn buses ran frequently from Leith to Princes Street, about a mile away in central Edinburgh, for a change of scenery.

Leith, like most seaports, had a multicultural community and anyone worth his salt could make a good living and be accepted there. Queen Victoria's mother was from the noble family of Saxe-Coburg & Gothe and when Victoria married her German cousin, Albert, in 1840 Germans became very much in fashion. Wilhelm had chosen well when he decided to settle in Leith.

❁　❁　❁　❁　❁

The following year, Wilhelm felt settled enough in his new surroundings to send to Hamburg for his fiancée. Johanna Catherina Maria Thiems arrived in Leith on June 17th, 1856 on the steamship *Best Bower*. They were married on June 26th and moved into their new home at 41 The Shore, across the street from the wharfs in Leith Harbour, as hotel keepers. Maria had been brought up to this way of life, as her parents owned a hotel in Hamburg, so it was a good beginning for their lives together. Over the next six years, they produced four children: Bertha, Dorothea Henrietta, Wilhelm Herrmann, and Albert.

In 1862, the Colterjahns moved to a house in prestigious North Leith, where Maria could concentrate on bringing up their family.

Wilhelm started, or joined, a ship chandler business at 46 The Shore and this was so successful that they took on ship provisioning as well. He and Maria next bought or built a big family home at 86 Ferry Road, among the wealthy merchants and professionals of North Leith, where they lived for the rest of their lives together. The final step was to apply for British citizenship. Wilhelm became a naturalized British subject on January 21st, 1870.

Leith treated the Colterjahns well and they prospered. The two sons went into the business with their father and the daughters found good husbands. Bertha married a master mariner from Russia, August Schlossmann, in 1873 and, over the years, they produced one son and five daughters. Dorothea Henrietta married a Scottish shipping clerk, Gilbert Archer Jamieson in 1885, but sadly died within a year of their marriage from septicemia. Albert married Catherine (Kate) McDonald Duncan from Rothsay in 1889, and they were blessed with three sons and one daughter. Albert was the only one of Wilhelm's children to carry on the Colterjahn name.

Wilhelm Herrmann never married but moved to Methil in Fife and started his own ship chandler business in partnership with Robert Taylor. Wilhelm died suddenly in July 1889 aged 28. Two years later, Albert bought out Robert Taylor, assumed the assets and liabilities of the business in Methil, and moved his family to live there.

✸   ✸   ✸   ✸   ✸

This was a century of intense patriotism and loyalty to their German-British Queen. It was an age of adventure with heroes who gave their lives for the Empire in mysterious, faraway lands. Wilhelm and Maria were proud grandparents and Wilhelm loved to tell the children stories of his days at sea on merchant ships in the Baltic. He repeated the tales he had heard of villainous pirates and selfless missionaries eaten by cannibals. Who better to hear these tales from than the captains who docked their ships at Leith, full of goods and travellers from all over the British Empire. The newspapers were filled with stories of famous men like General Gordon who died in Khartoum, Sudan and of Dr. Livingston's meeting with Mr. Stanley at the Victoria Falls in Africa; of the Indian Mutiny and the gold rush to California. In turn, Albert told these exciting tales to his children and they were passed on down the family.

It was also an age of invention. Practical uses for electricity were being developed throughout the 19th century, and this assisted the invention of long distance communication. In 1865, telegraph wires stretched across America from coast to coast, and about 11 years later Alexander Graham Bell invented the telephone. The Suez Canal opened in November 1869 after ten years of construction, cutting the route to India by about 7,000 kilometres. In 1883, Sir Sandford Fleming synchronized clocks around the world and in 1885, the Canadian Pacific Railway crossed Canada from Nova Scotia to British Columbia.

When the Pacific & Orient introduced the first cruise ship, the shipbuilding industry in both the Clyde and the Firth of Forth at Leith became a frenzy of activity, with the construction of new and bigger docks. These ships became floating hotels with every luxury available and created massive employment opportunities. Wilhelm Colterjahn & Sons Ship Chandlers were in the right place at the right time.

❀   ❀   ❀   ❀   ❀

On March 31st, 1899, Martin Ferdinand Wilhelm Colterjahn died of an abdominal tumour aged 70. He had led an interesting and successful life, loved and honoured by a large family. The early death of two of his children must have been heartbreaking, but Bertha and Albert had produced ten grandchildren between them, enough to keep his dreams of a dynasty alive. After his death, his widow, Maria, went to live with their daughter, Bertha and her husband. By this time, most of Bertha's children had grown up and left home. Albert and Kate had moved to Bo'ness to raise their family, and he eventually became the harbour master there.

A great era came to a close with the turn of the century and the death of Queen Victoria on January 22nd, 1901. War was on everyone's mind. The Second Anglo-Boer War in South Africa was killing British soldiers. 1905 brought the Russian Revolution, 1910 the Mexican Revolution, and 1911 the Chinese Revolution. The world was destabilizing everywhere. The Colterjahn family decided to follow the current trend and Anglicized their name to Colterjohn; Wilhelm became William and Erik changed to Eric. It was the final step in becoming truly British.

On July 28, 1914, Europe finally erupted into what was to become the Great War. Albert's four children participated with British patriotism. Wilhelm III (Bill) was 23 years old and enlisted in the 9th Royal Scots to fight against Germany, the country of his family's origins. He served in Europe where he was wounded and decorated. Jean McNicoll was a trained nurse and worked in this capacity during the war. Samuel John Duncan had attended the Heriot Watt Engineering College in Edinburgh and joined the army as an engineer. One of his postings was to protect the Forth Bridge and the naval bases around it. Albert Eric was only 14 years old when war was declared. He completed his schooling, joined the cadets, and enrolled in the Heriot Watt Engineering College, where he graduated as an electrical engineer in 1920.

The Great War, intended to be the war to end all wars, finally came to a conclusion on November 11th, 1918. The world was a changed place. Even in victory, there was a sense of loss and bitterness. It had left nine million combatants and seven million civilians dead. Millions more were crippled or left permanently damaged from poisonous gases. Unemployment was rife, even among those who returned fit enough to work. The social order and moral attitudes had changed and an era of confusion and euphoria gripped Britain and Europe.

❀　❀　❀　❀　❀

Bill (Wilhelm III) decided to emigrate and sailed from Glasgow on *SS Sicilian,* arriving in Montreal, Canada on May 13th, 1920 with his father's blessing and his mother's bible. He made a good life as an accountant for himself and his Canadian wife, Helen Andersen, but they never had any children. Two months later, his mother, Kate, died of a perforated carcinoma of the stomach followed by peritonitis. Albert continued to live in Bo'ness until he retired as harbour master, then he moved to Edinburgh to be closer to his daughter, Jean. Samuel John Duncan and Albert Eric, both engineers, found work where they could, but felt unsettled.

Sam, disenchanted with post-war Britain, eventually took an engineering appointment in Shanghai and sailed on May 25th, 1926. He found his new life so exciting that he looked for a job for his brother too. Eric sailed from London bound for Shanghai on June 15th, 1928. He also said goodbye to his girl-friend, Amy. She joined him in Shanghai the following year, but there is no record of whether they were engaged or not be-fore he left.

One can only imagine the emotions felt by Albert Col-terjohn, on saying farewell to his third son, as he left for Shanghai to join Sam. The family had barely sunk its roots into Scottish soil when their sons took off once more for foreign lands. His wife, Kate, had died, Bill had settled into his new life in Canada, Sam had gone to China, and now all he had left was his daughter, Jean. She was a nurse, working in Edinburgh, and would care for him for the rest of his life.

Albert and Kate had bred strong, healthy, well-educated children who had followed the call to excitement and adven-ture. They had been brought up on tales of empire and the co-lonial life, so it is hardly surprising. In fact, the three Col-terjohn boys were part of an early *brain drain* that sent well-educated Scots, especially engineers, all over the world to seek their fortunes.

❀ ❀ ❀ ❀ ❀

My name is Eric Duncan Colterjohn. Martin Ferdinand Wilhelm Colterjahn was my great-grandfather, Albert my grandfather and Albert Eric my father. They are my family and this is our story.

SHANGHAI: PANDORA'S BOX
1800 - 1900

During the hundred years that Shanghai developed as a treaty port, this great metropolis became the most corrupt, decadent, squalid, fun-loving and wealth-seeking city that modern civilization has ever witnessed. Born of greed, fueled by opium and swelled by fortune hunters and refugees from all over the world, Shanghai was without restraint. Almost everything was legal and morality was irrelevant. In a continuous cycle of boom and bust, fortunes were made and lost to every kind of deal, vice and depravity known to man. Everyone, foreigners and Chinese alike, was there to make money; lots of it, and as fast as possible.

Shanghai had what it took - a location that would sooner or later make it a very major trading port. Located half way up the coast of China on the Whangpoo (Huangpu) River, as it flows into the delta of the mighty Yangtze, it has safe anchorage for large ships and protection from the typhoons and subtropical storms that blow in from the East China Sea. The climate is reasonably temperate, with cold winters and hot steamy summers, but preferable to the extremes of temperature that most of the Chinese coastal cities experience. The Yangtze is listed as the third longest river in the world, flowing 3,100 miles across Asia from its source in Tibet to the Pacific Ocean, so provides easy access to the interior of China. It is literally the main highway of a vast empire of 700,000 square miles and an enormous population.

Shanghai is, however, barely above sea level and originally consisted of spongy mudflats. Surrounded by extremely fertile land, it was more suited to rice paddies than the construction of a vast modern metropolis, but that is what it eventually became. It developed early as an important harbor for the junks that plied their trade up and down the coast of China, several centuries before any European ships discovered it. A city slowly developed and, by the 16th century, a high surrounding wall had been built to guard against marauding Japanese pirates.

By the 18th century, the city had expanded beyond the walls and was starting to attract the interest of Europeans searching for trading opportunities, especially the British, Spanish, Portuguese, Dutch and French. In 1793, King George III of England sent a message to the Emperor of China requesting an opportunity to develop commercial relations, but was rejected. The industrial revolution was well established in Britain by then, and she badly needed new markets for her manufactured goods, and Chinese silk and cotton to feed her mills. As the British upper classes and the new industrial barons began to reap the benefits of this era of affluence, their tastes became more sophisticated. Their demand for luxurious goods and delicacies, like Chinese tea, porcelain, and fine fabrics, were hard to satisfy. The rumoured riches of China were an irresistible challenge as it was believed to be a cornucopia of desirable treasures. Britain was desperate, not only to find a way to trade with China, but also to be the first Western nation to do so, thus controlling the way the future developed.

Britain's power in India was spreading by this time, and she had fallen heir to vast opium fields, especially in Bengal and Malwa, and these were to provide the answer to her problems. Two adventurous Scots, William Jardine and James Matheson, keen to be forerunners in the scramble for trade with China, proposed to the British government that they trade the opium from India for the goods that they so badly wanted from China. The only problem was that, by 1800, the Chinese emperor had banned the import, sale and use of opium, so that it could not be introduced into China directly. Instead, they developed an army of middlemen, Chinese *country traders* as they became known, who relieved the British ships of their illicit cargo at sea or from Indian ports, and stored it in depots near Canton. From there, the opium was smuggled up the coast and rivers in fast ships and distributed all over China. This was an immediate success and quickly became the most valuable commercial crop of its time, creating huge fortunes for Britain and many other countries. By the end of the 1830s, 12 million Chinese were smoking opium and Jardine Matheson & Company were supplying one third of all the opium that was imported into China. The emperor and his government were powerless to stop its expansion.

❀ ❀ ❀ ❀ ❀

The steadily increasing importation of opium was creating many social and health problems, while draining the Chinese coffers and bringing the threat of bankruptcy to the government in Peking. In 1839, the emperor was sufficiently outraged to send an opium suppression commissioner to Canton. Foreign merchants were confined to their premises and their opium stocks seized and destroyed. The British welcomed this state of confrontation. William Jardine immediately sailed for Britain to organize a powerful lobby of industrialists, city bankers and merchants to petition the British Foreign Office to take action against China. Jardine supplied his personal maps and local experience to assist the British to develop a strategy for a full-scale military campaign and to demand that the emperor open up some northern ports to foreign trade. When the war resolution was passed, Jardine Matheson & Company leased some of their ships, pilots and translators to the invading force.

The British captured Shanghai in June 1842, and the Treaty of Nanking, (the first of the Unequal Treaties in China) was signed on board a British gunboat on August 29. As a result of this First Opium War, the Chinese emperor was fined 21 million silver dollars and the Island of Hong Kong was ceded to the United Kingdom in perpetuity. Five British treaty ports were established at Shanghai, Canton, Ningpo, Fuchow, and Amoy, with provisions for foreign settlements and concessions. French and American concessions followed soon afterwards. Foreigners, party to these treaties and who lived in these treaty port cities, enjoyed legal extraterritorial privileges. Essentially, this meant that they were subject to the laws of their home nations, rather than the laws of China, and developed their own courts and law enforcement agencies, creating a colony type situation on Chinese territorial soil. This was without doubt an extremely severe penalty to China, and greatly undermined the integrity of the Ch'ing Dynasty. The British received everything that they had wanted and more, even to negotiating a *most-favoured nation* clause in the treaty. This provided for all nations who were party to the treaty to be given the same privileges and rights as the host country, China, including low tariffs, which proved of enormous benefit over the years to come.

❀   ❀   ❀   ❀   ❀

When the first British merchants and settlers arrived in Shanghai in 1843, they were given 140 acres of low muddy land fronting on the west and north banks of the Whangpoo River, north of the Chinese walled city. This established the British Settlement, later to become the International Settlement, and from the first was administered by the British. A year later, both the French and the American governments received land that provided them with smaller areas for concessions.

The newcomers pitched their tents and immediately started to construct docks, warehouses and rudimentary housing, but every building had to be supported by pylons driven deep into the mud to find bedrock. The foreign population of Shanghai did not reach one hundred until 1848, but the port grew quickly to succeed Canton as China's biggest and busiest international port. The Americans were given an area in Hongkew, to the north of the British across the Soochow Creek but, as this was away from the prime areas of development, most decided they would prefer to live in the British section. The land was cheaper in Hongkew, so this eventually became home to middle-class Chinese who could not afford to live in the more fashionable parts of the International Settlement. Numerous different ethnic groups also settled there over the years, when they first arrived in Shanghai. The Japanese gradually took over a large part of Hongkew, which became known as Little Tokyo. The language, culture and way of life of this area were completely Japanese. Other nationals rarely went there except to enjoy the restaurants.

In the following 10 years Shanghai became the fastest growing city in the world. People from many countries arrived to service the expanding population and to make their fortune. The noise of pylons being driven into the mud continued night and day, as construction teams tried to keep up with the demand. One by one the original shacks were torn down to make way for new permanent buildings. In the International Settlement, the residential areas were slowly moved west and the Bund, along the riverfront, became the most prestigious commercial location. Banks, trading houses, shipping offices and the Palace Hotel settled into enormous stone neo-classic structures, more suited to the ancient cities of Europe than to this developing seaport, but the finest of them all was the Shanghai Club. They were determined that this would be the equal of any men's club in the world. A church, shops and entertainment facilities were built and even a racetrack. There was a sports field in the center of this for polo and cricket and a bridle path around the outside. Life in Shanghai was slowly emulating the British colonial way, and there was lots of money to support this extravagant lifestyle.

❀ ❀ ❀ ❀ ❀

In 1851 the Taiping Rebellion broke out in protest against the corrupt and ineffective Manchu Government causing violent civil war throughout China. Their leader, a Christian fanatic, believed in a "Heaven Kingdom" where God owned all and every man was equal. While the Taiping armies ravaged, pillaged and massacred hundreds of thousands of Chinese civilians over the next 13 years, it was more or less business as usual in Shanghai. Although foreigners preferred not to become involved, they had to help defend the city on several occasions when they were threatened, and employed mercenaries to protect their property. Three hundred thousand refugees flooded into the city looking for protection, and caused a major real estate boom. Many of these new arrivals were wealthy businessmen who brought their capital with them and were happy to pay high rents and invest in Shanghai enterprises.

In 1860, the old emperor died and, as his heir was still a small child, the empress dowager took over control of the country. She was weak, greedy and very much against modernization, industrialization and everything foreign. The officials around her were corrupt and the strong government that was so much needed at this time of civil war was not there. Concurrently, the escalating Second Opium War came to a head that year, when Westerners attacked the Summer Palace in Peking and burned it to the ground. This resulted in the Treaty of Tientsing, which gave important benefits to the victorious foreigners, providing them with the right to travel legally anywhere in China and the opening of four new treaty ports inland. In response, the dowager empress insisted on imposing a tax on opium, not realizing that this would, in effect, be condoning it officially. With the mighty Yangtze River open to foreign ships, and the advent of steamships in the China Seas, all the prizes of the interior of China were now there for the taking. The lid was off Pandora's Box and the genies of avarice and lust were set free.

The timing was propitious for the merchants of Shanghai as the American Civil War broke out in 1861, cutting off cotton supplies to the weaving mills in England. This gave a huge boost to the cotton growers and exporters around Shanghai.

With not only trade, but also the population exploding, the Shanghai Municipal Council was established in 1863 by the British residents to administer the International Settlement. The French Concession followed soon after with a similar arrangement, administered by the French consul. By this time, the two foreign enclaves had expanded to three times their original sizes and the port was now the sixth largest in the world. It also had 688 brothels and too many opium and gaming houses to count.

As the civil war finally drew to an end, it brought with it the first recession in Shanghai. Many of the refugees returned to their towns and villages leaving whole streets of the city unoccupied and bankrupting landlords. However, this was short lived as some of the vacating merchants decided to leave their capital invested in Shanghai businesses, and this encouraged other wealthy Chinese from neighboring cities to do the same. This was the beginning of the pattern for the future, with joint ventures developing between Chinese and Westerners.

❋   ❋   ❋   ❋   ❋

Meanwhile, Japan was once again looking for a way to get a more permanent foothold on Chinese soil and declared war on China, ostensibly over Korea. Aware of the growing influence of Europeans in China, Japan felt that it was time to share in their many privileges. Although China had a greater number of ships, she could not compete with the technical superiority of the Japanese, and lost the first Sino-Japanese War.

The following Treaty of Shimonoseki in 1894 was to have far-reaching effects, not only in China, but for Britain and Europe too. This treaty provided for the Japanese acquisition of a number of Chinese territories, including Taiwan and the Penghu (Pescadores) Islands, and China was required to recognize the full independence of Korea. However, the real prize for Japan was the access to several treaty ports in China with all the benefits that the Westerners were enjoying under the terms of the Unequal Treaties. To these, Japan also negotiated the right to build and operate industrial plants, finally defeating the Manchu government's ban. Under the *Most Favoured Nation* clause in the treaty, all other countries party to the Unequal Treaties were now able to do the same. Japan had finally obtained the legal right to trade, settle, travel and manufacture on Chinese soil with the same low tariffs as the Chinese.

Immediately, most of the 18 or 20 treaty participants started to build factories and manufacture a large number of products. Once again, Shanghai was surmounting a boom. This was hard on local Chinese industry which did not have the technology or equipment of the Western countries. From now on, foreigners in China were able to export manufactured goods, not just the raw materials, which had a devastating effect on industry in Britain, America and all other industrial countries. This started a trend that is still true today.

Shanghai: Politics and Power
1842 - 1826

From the very beginning, enterprising Chinese found ways of making money from, or alongside, their invaders. As the foreigners became wealthy, so did many Chinese. However, there was no social communication between the two groups and Chinese were excluded from the Westerners' clubs, parks and even the racetrack, except as servants, so a parallel social order developed, in many cases emulating the facilities of the foreign residents. Even when a Chinese built an enormous house next to a wealthy foreigner in the International Settlement, there would be no, or very little, social relationship. Initially, the Chinese were content to make money and found the social habits of the Westerners strange and often unacceptable. However, the children of these wealthy Chinese were well educated, indeed they were often sent abroad for this, and resented being second-class citizens in their own country. This is fully understandable, and was similar to the pattern emerging all over the colonized world by the end of the 1800s.

The growing resentment of the expanding Chinese middle class was not only towards the foreigners, but also to their own Manchu government. When Shanghai developed the first modern printing press and publishing industry in China, many of the young elite moved to the International Settlement to wage a *war of words,* hoping for immunity by living there.

In 1898, a group of peasants, belonging to a secret society in northern China known as the Boxers, rose in protest against the Manchu government and all foreign influence, in what became known as the Boxer Rebellion. When the dowager empress backed the Boxers, they came in from the country and attacked foreign legations in Peking. Western nations sent a large force to protect their nationals and safeguard their investments in China, but it took almost two years to subdue hostilities with great loss of life on both sides. It almost bankrupted the Manchu government and weakened the power and influence of the Ch'ing (Qing) Dynasty further.

By now, 95 per cent of the residents of the International Settlement were Chinese, many owning their own homes and businesses and paying taxes on an equal basis with the foreigners. Several requests for Chinese representation on the Shanghai Municipal Council were rejected so, in 1902, they formed the Chinese Chamber of Commerce. This was to play a large part in providing a focal point for Chinese ambitions and resentments. At the same time, a very strong anti-American feeling was developing, due to the refusal of the US government to rescind the Exclusion Act. This had been passed in 1882 to control the number of Chinese immigrants to America and restricted their rights as residents. This was causing discrimination and great hardship to many Chinese abroad. By 1905, the Chinese in Shanghai had placed a boycott on everything American, and even some servants would not work for American households. This soon spread to the rest of China but the act was not repealed until 1943. The boycott slowly slackened, as it was interfering with trade, but the resentment remained.

Between 1895 and 1910 the population of Shanghai doubled, and by 1930 it had tripled. Unrest all over China was widespread, so it was not unexpected when the Wuchang Uprising of the New National Army erupted in 1911, spreading through the country like wildfire. The Ch'ing Dynasty, which had ruled China since 1644, was overthrown and the dowager empress and the boy emperor were sent into exile. China was now a republic, but the generals and warlords continued to fight amongst themselves for the next few decades, providing very unstable government.

In spite of this, the revolution gave the population a sense of liberation from the backward Manchu rule, and Western ideas and standards started to spread throughout the country. A new generation of intellectuals, under the leadership of Dr. Sun Yat-sen, keen to create a strong, modern China became politically involved. Women felt freer to leave the compounds of their homes, stopped binding their feet, and were able to seek an education. The workers exchanged the long blue gowns for blue cotton trousers and short jackets, and pigtails on men were outlawed. Modernization was slowly happening. Although China was still far from being a democracy, Sun Yat-sen was strongly influenced by Western ways and thinking, as he realized that this was necessary to compete in a modern world. His new provisional government followed the American example of a written constitution, and their legal system was copied from England.

❀ ❀ ❀ ❀ ❀

Only three years after the revolution, war ravaged Europe. A large number of the foreigners in China left to support their various countries, leaving a caretaker group of older people to protect their interests, and many of the businesses were left in the charge of Chinese compradors and managers. With the exodus of these Westerners, both wealthy Chinese and Japanese recognized their opportunity and flooded into Shanghai to start new businesses and factories. By 1915, Japan had more nationals in Shanghai than any other foreign country. A few years later, those foreigners who returned, found a much changed city. Thousands of White Russians had arrived after the Bolshevik War, many of them destitute and desperate for work, providing cheap labor in all fields. As Russia had renounced her Unequal Treaty rights after the Bolshevik Revolution, these immigrants did not have extraterritoriality. This meant that they had none of the privileges enjoyed by most of the other foreigners in Shanghai, although many of them came from noble backgrounds.

The Great War had started a social revolution in Europe and around the world that would take another world war and a further twenty years to complete. However, to the Shanghailanders (foreigners in Shanghai), nothing had changed, at least on a personal level. Western *taipans* found themselves mixing more freely with wealthy Chinese businessmen, but most of the foreign-owned clubs and areas of prestige were still closed to Chinese, even of the highest rank, and they still did not mix socially. One exception to this was the Shanghai Race Club, which finally opened its doors to everyone after the war. Admittedly, this was for economic reasons rather than from a sense of largess. To the Westerners, this was just the way it was. However, the Chinese had expected that things would change once the war ended, even hoping for the return of the treaty ports to China. It is no wonder resentment against foreign domination escalated, but most foreigners seemed totally oblivious to this.

After the Great War, Sun Yat-sen appealed to both Britain and the United States to send advisers to China to help unify the country and provide a strong central government. Britain was struggling with enormous problems of her own in the aftermath of the war, and the USA felt her priorities lay in the rehabilitation of war-torn Europe. Both countries turned China down. They continued to defend the rights of their nationals in the treaty ports, and to support their enormously lucrative trade with China, but could see no benefits in becoming involved with China as a whole. When, in 1919, the Treaty of Versailles awarded the leased territories confiscated from the Germans to the Japanese, China's oldest enemy, this was the final humiliation. It was a serious blow to Chinese pride and sense of growing nationalism, and demonstrated once again how insensitive the Europeans were to Chinese interests.

In 1918, the Chinese government had made the importation, sale and use of opium illegal. This immediately took opium out of the control of more or less responsible merchants, sent it underground and put it into the hands of gangsters. They took Shanghai by storm and gradually added organized gambling, arms dealing, and every other form of vice to their areas of control.

By 1920, the whole of China was in chaos. There was no proper national government, in spite of the efforts Sun Yat-sen's growing Kuomintang party. Competing warlords, with nothing but self-interest in mind, took over the government of most of the cities from 1916 to 1926, except the foreign concessions, and they joined forces with the underworld. Shanghai, being the opium capital of China, attracted large numbers of gangsters. The infamous Green Gang rose to the top by developing a drug cartel that was so huge that they were able to infiltrate the police in the foreign concessions and even bribed the garrisons. Things got so out of control that eventually the Shanghai Municipal Council made an attempt to clean up the International Settlement but, with three separate jurisdictions in Shanghai, the offenders only had to cross the road into the French Concession or into one of the Chinese-administered areas.

As Britain, USA and even Germany had turned their backs on China when asked for help, Sun Yat-sen finally sent Chiang Kai-shek to Moscow to approach Stalin. Chiang succeeded in his mission, but that time spent in Russia would instil a deep fear of communism in him that would strongly influence his attitudes in the future. In 1923, Soviet Russia pledged aid to China and, within two years, over a thousand Soviet military and political advisers were active in China. The following year, Chiang opened the Whampoa Military Academy in Canton, the first of its kind in China, with Russian help.

On the whole, this did not have much effect on the foreign community who continued to prosper in business and industry, and dine, dance or gamble well into the small hours of the mornings. Shanghai was the jazz capital of the world by then, American movies were the rage, and the city was full of dance halls, cabarets, nightclubs and other forms of amusement, often run by the very talented White Russians. Consumed by their frenetic life of privilege, most of the Westerners were unaware of, or simply did not care about, the growing discontent in the Chinese parts of the city surrounding them. The conditions of labor, especially in the factories, were appalling with long hours, minimal pay and inhuman working environments.

⊛　⊛　⊛　⊛　⊛

The Chinese Communist Party officially started in 1921, and trade unions were soon formed to tackle the terrible labor conditions. Communism was spreading fast in Europe, particularly on an intellectual level, and many aspiring young Chinese communists went to Europe to be educated, especially in Paris and Moscow. Most of these well-educated and idealistic young people returned home to form the nucleus of the new Communist party, and brought new ideas and hope to the struggling Chinese people. Resentment continued to grow as the emerging Chinese middle class remained second class citizens in their own country, in spite of their education and western philosophies. At the same time, the early 1920s saw a constant struggle for power between rival warlords in both the cities and the countryside. In Shanghai, the Green Gang steadily gained strength, ruling the underworld and influencing every aspect of city life.

On May 30th, 1925, 3,000 workers, reacting to an incident in a Japanese factory, demonstrated against Western imperialism, Japanese superiority and the Unequal Treaties. Both Westerners and Japanese were terrified and fired on unarmed demonstrators, causing an enormous number of deaths. A general strike broke out the following day and was supported by 117 unions with over 200,000 members, with costs underwritten by the Chinese General Chamber of Commerce. Resentful of their foreign competitors' privileged status, wealthy Chinese bankers and businessmen were delighted to show their patriotism, and within days all Japanese and Western-owned factories had closed down. Almost all the services to the International Settlement were shut off and foreign ships were left unloaded. Japanese and Western factory owners and businessmen had to stand by while their Chinese competitors capitalized on the situation.

On June 6, the foreign controlled Shanghai Municipal Council shut down the electricity to the Chinese factories in the International Settlement and in Yangtzepoo in retaliation. This quickly brought the Chinese bankers and financial supporters of the strike to withdraw their support and a settlement was negotiated. However, the general strike had spread to 28 other cities, with the worst situation in Canton and Hong Kong, which lasted for 16 months.

While the Communists were organizing strikes all over the country, the Kuomintang was having its own problems. Sun Yat-sen died in March, 1925, creating internal havoc within the party. In an attempt to show party unity, the Kuomintang declared itself the Nationalist Government of China in July 1925. A fierce leadership battle ensued with Chiang Kai-shek emerging as the commander-in-chief of the Nationalist Revolutionary Army. A year later, he launched his Northern Expedition, a military campaign to defeat and banish the warlords and reduce foreign imperialism. This had been Sun Yat-sen's great ambition.

It was into this volatile political environment, that my uncle, Samuel John Duncan Colterjohn, a young Scottish engineer, found himself when he arrived in Shanghai in the summer of 1926.

A SLOW BOAT TO CHINA

1926 – 1927

As the Peninsular & Oriental steamship *Kashmir* sailed across the East China Sea and entered the estuary of the Yangtze River, one can imagine the mounting excitement of the passengers. She was only five and a half thousand tons and had sailed all the way from London to Shanghai, leaving on May 25th, 1926. Most of the passengers were going to jobs, and many of them returning after a home leave. There were 95 people separated into two classes, including eight couples, 58 unaccompanied men, 11 women and eight children. All of them, except one woman, were British.

The majority of the passengers travelled by second class, but there were a few of the best cabins kept for those prominent or wealthy enough to pay for a little more comfort and extra service. They came with a wide range of occupations and skills from bankers and merchants to missionaries, teachers and clerks to engineers and archeologists, only to mention a few. Several of the women were on their way to be married, some traveling with a chaperone. There were journalists and some adventuresome travelers on their way around the world. Undoubtedly, amongst them were a few opportunists who had already made easy money from other passengers at the card tables each night. They all had one thing in common: they were full of anticipation and excitement to have finally reached Shanghai; the most exotic port of them all.

Sam Colterjohn, my uncle, was a mechanical engineer and had been hired as works manager by the Anderson, Meyer Company. Vilhelm Meyer had arrived in Shanghai in 1902 where, a few years later, he founded a company that was to become one of the largest in China. Initially, it specialized in the import of building materials – iron, steel and glass. When the First World War closed down European supply markets, Meyer placed his orders with the United States, where he also found new capital and new partners. Andersen, Meyer & Co. thus became an American corporation, registered in New York, and the General Electric Company's sole agent in China. In 1921, they built a new factory in Shanghai providing superior working conditions, and manufactured domestic appliances and fans. Sam knew this would be a challenging job and was looking forward to it.

※   ※   ※   ※   ※

The trip out took five to six weeks and they visited many famous ports, each with their own special character, flavors and smells. After leaving England, they almost certainly had a couple of rough days in the Atlantic before passing the Rock of Gibraltar and sailing through the quiet seas of the Mediterranean, stopping at Naples or Malta and possibly at Alexandria. From there, they entered the Suez Canal at Port Said, and this miracle of engineering would have fascinated those doing it for the first time. Port Said was a wonderful place to shop. The famous emporium of Simon Arts was full of unusual items from both the Middle East and Europe to tempt travelers.

The port also offered the irresistible fun of bartering with the merchants in the *bumboats*, selling everything from oriental carpets to gem stones, many of doubtful provenance. These were little boats, laden to the gunnels with every imaginable form of merchandise, which floated around the cruise ships. The passengers would lean over the rails of the ships and bargain for anything they wanted. The merchant would throw up a rope for the customer to catch and then send the goods up in a basket. If the passenger wished to buy an item, the money went down the same way.

A number of people disembarked at Port Sudan, half way down the Red Sea, likely traveling to Khartoum or to one of the many desert archeological sites. Leaving the canal at the south end, they called at Aden to take on water and supplies. From there, as they crossed the Arabian Sea to Bombay, they were greeted by flocks of seabirds and exotic smells while still many miles out at sea. The passengers were given a day in this gateway to the Orient to explore the city, with its long history and exciting places to visit. Sailing south, they called at the port of Colombo, in Ceylon, and travelled up the east coast of India to Calcutta. They then headed south, through the Bay of Bengal and the Indian Ocean to Penang and Singapore. The final stretch took them into the South China Sea to Hong Kong and then north to Shanghai. In each port, some of the passengers disembarked with a few new ones joining the ship for the final days of the voyage.

These trips were never dull, even on the long sea days. The *Old China Hands*, returning after home leave, spent many hours talking about China and giving the new boys an education on what to expect, as most of them had only a very basic idea of what China was like. These were foreigners who had lived there for so long that their life in China had become part of their identity. They came from all walks of life and could be missionaries or mercenaries, bankers or merchants. They were often British, but not necessarily so, and occasionally some of them even stopped taking their furloughs, especially if they no longer had family to return to in their home country. China became their home.

There were lectures on the geography, history and the social customs of the Far East, given by those passengers who knew the country well, and some lessons on local dialects and Pidgin English. These were people going out to a new and exciting life, or returning to one they loved, so life in Shanghai was their main topic of conversation. The few travelers were as anxious as any to learn what they could before arriving at their destination. And, life was not all work. There were bands and entertainers onboard, with good food, plenty to drink and dancing into the small hours of the morning. Above all, they made friends and business contacts who gave them a good start in this foreign land. When air travel took over from these ships in the 1960s, the newcomers found themselves dumped into an alien culture with little preparation, and none of the advantages of a *Slow Boat to China*.

❀   ❀   ❀   ❀   ❀

A short distance into the Yangtze, Captain Stringer slowed the engines and the ship gradually turned south into the mouth of the Whuangpoo River. Sam Colterjohn stood with the other passengers on deck, watching with mounting excitement as they covered the twelve short miles into Shanghai. The first signs of the approaching city were large brick factories, warehouses, godowns and commercial docks on both sides of the river in the industrial areas of Yangtzepoo and Pootung, as the ship twisted with a big, slow bend in the river. There were steel foundries and lumberyards, cotton mills and shipyards. There were huge billboards with pictures of beautiful girls advertising everything from cigarettes and whiskey to Chinese wonder drugs. Next was a long procession of warships from half a dozen nations, proudly displaying their flags, anchored in the middle of the river and keeping a watchful eye. Finally, with one more curve of the river, the full face of Shanghai came into sight.

Nothing had prepared Sam for the sheer grandeur and magnificence of the famous Bund. First, there was the dignified, granite edifice of the British Consulate by the Soochow Creek, and the public gardens in front of it running almost down to the water's edge. From there, stretching in one incredible, mile-long crescent, were huge buildings in every architectural style, from granite and marble neo-classic columns and pediments to Moorish arches and modern Art Deco.

Finally, the Bund culminated at the south end with a flourish of Italian Renaissance, the most impressive building of them all, the Shanghai Club. Between these two bastions of British prestige, were the customs building with its famous clock tower, the Hong Kong Shanghai Bank flanked by a pair of larger-than-life bronze lions, and numerous head offices of shipping lines, insurances companies and financial houses. On the corners where the Nanking Road met the Bund, were two big hotels. The Palace was the gracious old lady, constructed in 1908, on the south side. The Cathay Hotel, occupying part of the new Sassoon Building on the north corner, was still under construction at this point, but was to become the most luxurious, modern hotel to be found anywhere in Asia.

The street in front of these buildings was chaos 24 hours a day, as Shanghai never slept. The early morning saw drunken sailors and revelers making their way home after a night of parties or gambling in chauffeured cars, rickshaws or by foot, colliding with peasants bringing their livestock and vegetables to market. These would usually be carried on both ends of long poles, with everything from a trussed pig at one end to a basket of cabbages at the other. Young mothers struggled along with heavy loads, often carrying babies and toddlers strapped to their backs. Tired sing-song girls and courtesans competed for transport with foreign clerks in pinstriped suits on their way to work.

Construction vehicles, loaded to unsafe heights, pushed past private cars, rickshaws and anyone and anything that got in their way. Flower-sellers and vendors pulling barrows of hot food blocked every corner. In the middle of all of this, cyclists, pedestrians and beggars weaved in and out of the vehicles, trying to reach a thousand destinations. Traffic policemen stood on drums at the intersections in all this turmoil, trying to direct the traffic, but it was almost a useless task. The picture changed a little in color and shape as the day developed but the frenzy, noise and smells never ceased.

Across the street, there was a broad grassy area along the river where those at leisure could stroll and watch the pageantry of daily life unfold. The waterfront itself was as chaotic as the street, with every size and shape of boat imaginable. Junks and sampans not only offered transport, but also performed an infinite number of uses from high-class restaurants to dirty brothels and gaming dens. Some poor Chinese raised their families and lived their whole lives on sampans, anchored in the mouth of the Soochow Creek. The wharfs at either end of the Bund provided berths for the smaller ships and docking for the tenders from those anchored in the center of the river. As the Whuangpoo was still tidal in Shanghai, the flotsam and jetsam of the big city went out on one tide, often to return on the next. This would include coffins, corpses, dead animals and every form of domestic garbage known to man. Shanghai was very advanced in many of the technologies like electricity and the telephone, but was a long way behind most European cities in the disposal of its waste.

My Uncle Sam must have been totally amazed as he waited for the representative from his company, who made him welcome and took him to temporary lodgings. The scene he was witnessing was beyond his wildest imagination.

THE SHANGHAI MASSACRE

1927

In the summer of 1926, while Sam was settling into his new life in Shanghai, the political situation must have appeared quiet and stable to him, especially as he lived and worked in the International Settlement. However, at exactly this time, Chiang Kai-shek, having taken over as commander-in-chief of the Nationalist Revolutionary Army, launched his Northern Expedition to crush the warlords, forming a united front with the Communists. From Canton, he moved north taking one city after another with comparative ease. The Communists went ahead with propaganda and captured the hearts and minds of the people, so there was very little actual fighting, and the army developed confidence and a new sense of nationalism. They arrived in Hankow in January 1927, where an anti-imperialist mob forced the foreigners to surrender their concessions. They then moved on to Kiukiang and Nanking where they did the same thing.

It was a wonderful example of what could be achieved when the Kuomintang and the Communists put political differences aside and worked together, but this co-operation was not to last much longer. It was also the first time the foreigners in China had to face the realities of their privileged status in a growing mood of nationalism.

With the army now poised to attack Shanghai next, the 70,000 foreigners panicked and many wives and families were evacuated. Although the primary purpose of the Northern Expedition was to defeat and banish the warlords still governing the major cities, success had increased the sense of nationalism and resentment of foreign domination in Chinese of all political persuasions. The Shanghailanders (foreigners) had just cause to feel threatened. Forty thousand troops arrived from a dozen countries to protect foreign interests and barricaded the International Settlement and the French Concession, making them an island surrounded by hostile Chinese demanding, not only the banishment of the warlords, but also the abolition of the Unequal Treaties and foreign privilege.

The Communists moved into the Chinese parts of the city and followed their established plan of agitating the workers and preparing for the arrival of the Nationalist Army. However, Chiang Kai-shek, feeling that he no longer needed the help of the Communists, broke off diplomatic relations with Soviet Russia, and delayed his march into Shanghai. The first two calls to a general strike failed, and the Shanghai Municipal Council started negotiations with the trade unions to calm things down. In January they created the Shanghai Provisional Court to try Chinese residents in the International Settlement with Chinese magistrates, and in February they approved the appointment of three Chinese members to the Council. This offer was rejected as insufficient, but it opened the doors to more co-operation. However, this was not enough to reduce the threat of the Communists, whose ranks were growing daily, and in February, 1927 terrified bankers and businessmen, both Chinese and foreign, offered Chiang Kai-shek three million dollars to suppress the Communist-inspired uprisings and to set up new Nationalist headquarters in Nanking. Thus, Chiang abandoned his former alliance with the Communists and became a temporary lackey of the imperial powers and wealthy Shanghainese (Chinese), while serving his own best long-term interests.

On March 21st, 1927 Chou En-lai personally organized a third general strike and over 800,000 workers walked out against the local government of warlords. The whole of Shanghai ground to a stop, and all Chinese parts of the city came under the control of the workers and Communist sympathizers.

Six days later, Chiang and his Nationalist army made a triumphal entry into Shanghai, where they were warmly greeted by the foreign community. The Green Gang also offered their support in exchange for protection of their monopoly of the opium trade. This created a most unholy trinity; the formation of an alliance of the foreign and Chinese bankers and businessmen, Chiang Kai-shek, and the Green Gang, leaders of the underworld. What followed was one of the most violent and bloody episodes in Shanghai's history and is known as the Shanghai Massacre.

On April 12th, Chiang started a purge of the Communists and labor unions, with wholesale slaughter of workers and students, especially at the Commercial Press's huge plant, which was the Communist command center. One hundred thousand citizens, including many women and children, paraded through the city to present a petition to the Nationalist military commander. They were gunned down in the streets and a search for survivors and Communist sympathizers went on for weeks. These were murdered, often with great cruelty and without a trial. In about three weeks, so many Chinese had been killed, men women and children, that there will never be an accurate account, but it certainly went into the tens of thousands, with decapitated corpses scattered throughout the Chinese parts of the city. From then on, Chiang became totally obsessed with the destruction of the Communists, in spite of the much greater growing threat of the Japanese. This vendetta lasted for more than 20 years and would culminate in the Nationalist Kuomintang Party's defeat by the Communists.

※　※　※　※　※

Chiang Kai-shek wasted no time in setting up his new headquarters in Nanking, which was no longer a treaty port, and expelled all the Russian advisers. At this point, he had control of the Nationalist army, but was not a leader of the party. A period of readjustment followed, while the various factions of the Nationalist Kuomintang Party reunited and competed for the leadership positions. Chiang wisely absented himself for a while, and was finally invited by the party to return to his post as commander of the army and was appointed to the Kuomintang's Central Executive Committee.

As the Chinese buried their dead and cleaned up the city, order was restored to the International Settlement. The foreign wives and families returned, factories reopened and businesses went back to work as usual. Chinese administration was strengthened by the creation of the Greater Shanghai Municipality, which combined all the Chinese parts of the city under the rule of a mayor appointed by the central government. Bankers and businessmen breathed a collective sigh of relief, at least for a while, but they were still not off the hook. Back in control of the army, Chiang once again demanded that they provide more funds to pay his troops and continue his military campaign. A reign of terror followed, where all who resisted his extortion and intimidation were kidnapped, tortured and often murdered. From the end of March until mid-June no wealthy Chinese was safe and a wave of kidnapping swept the city. The foreign *taipans* were not directly threatened, but the integrated mesh of their business dealings meant that no-one in Shanghai was immune from the demands of the Green Gang in Chiang's employ. When the Kuomintang announced the sale of government bonds, no business of any importance dared to refuse to purchase them. Through these and other unorthodox methods, Chiang acquired about 50 million dollars for his war chest.

He now turned to rewarding those who had served him loyally and well and Tu Yuen-sen, leader of the Green Gang was top of his list. Chiang awarded him an honorary rank of major general in the army at a ceremony in Nanking, and appointed Tu's associate, Chang Hsiao-lin, head of the Opium Suppression Bureau. This gave Tu, not only a monopoly on the illegal distribution and sale of all opium imports, but also the legal means of confiscating them. Although the government was opposed to narcotics trafficking, Chiang Kai-shek split the profits with Tu, ensuring an enormous, steady income for them both. After the Shanghai massacre, the foreign community had declared Tu a hero, for protecting their lives and property, so he now felt it was time to move from the underworld to respectable Shanghai society. He set himself up as a banker, philanthropist and consultant to anyone in need of protection or counseling. His wealth and influence were so great that he was immediately accepted. This was typical of how things worked in Shanghai!

Meanwhile, Chiang had positioned himself for social and political elevation. On the first of December, 1927 he married Soong Mei-ling from China's foremost Westernized, Christian family and sister of the widow of the much-loved Sun Yat-sen. This raised his standing with the foreign community, who flocked to attend the wedding, and also placed him at the top of the list of competitors for the leadership of the Kuomintang government. He arranged for Sun Yat-sen's remains to be moved from Peking to Nanking and, on June 1st, 1929, they were ceremonially enshrined in a marble mausoleum. This was now the official seat of the Nationalist Kuomintang Government and was recognized by countries all over the world.

❈   ❈   ❈   ❈   ❈

The events of 1927 must have been too violent and traumatic for the Shanghailanders to ignore, so it is an interesting point to consider. It is a recorded fact that many women and children were evacuated, mainly to Hong Kong, before the Massacre of Shanghai and that about 40,000 troops from a dozen countries were rushed in to protect the lives and property of foreigners and to barricade the International Settlement and the French Concession. However, it would be interesting to know just how the average foreigner, like Sam Colterjohn, felt and dealt with these events. Many visitors to Shanghai, some of them famous writers like Arthur Ransome, recorded their views on this subject and were astonished at the arrogance, complacency and lack of interest the foreigners had in events outside their small and privileged circle. Most of them appeared to have no interest at all in the China around them and, those who did, were usually disapproved of by their peers.

It seems that the usual attitude was to ask:

"Does the upheaval affect my business interests, my family or my social life?"

If the answer was "no", then it was of no interest to them and life went on as usual.

If the answer was "yes", then the next question was:

"Who do we pay to protect our interests and get rid of the problem?"

History certainly upholds this, and the lack of understanding and compassion for the Chinese outside their sphere of influence has been written about in many books and articles. However, it is hard to imagine someone like my Uncle Sam, who worked in industry, not to have been swept along in the events. His factory was located in the International Settlement, but the workers must have belonged to a union and would have responded to the call to strike. He left no record of his feelings from this time, but his actions speak for themselves. In spite of everything that happened, he felt secure enough in his life in Shanghai to encourage his younger brother, Eric, (my father) to join him the following year and helped him to find a job.

BECOMING SHANGHAILANDERS
1928 – 1930

O n June 15th, 1928 my father, Albert Eric Colterjohn, aged 28 and a graduate from the Heriot Watt Engineering College in Edinburgh, sailed from London on the P & O steamship *Rajputana* bound for Shanghai. His voyage followed the same course that took Sam east, but the *Rajputana* was almost twice the size of the *Kashmir*. This may well have cut a few days off the trip and provided more in the way of facilities and entertainment. Otherwise, the voyage out was very similar, and Eric enjoyed all the same emotions and excitement on arriving in Shanghai as his brother had done two years earlier. He had a job waiting for him as an electrical engineer with the Municipal Electricity Department and accommodation with Sam. With a warm welcome, an interesting and well paid job to provide a challenge, and the delights of the most fun-loving city in the world beckoning, we know that Eric settled into his new life with enthusiasm. There could hardly have been a more exciting place for two young bachelors to be anywhere in the world at that time.

In August of the following year, the Municipal Electricity Department was bought by a group of investors, mainly American, and the new company was incorporated as the Shanghai Power Company in Delaware, USA. This had been founded in 1882 as the Shanghai Electric Company, and had been bought by the municipality in 1893. As the city expanded, so did the importance of this essential utility, attracting interest from foreign investors. This further secured Eric's future as he was appointed to the post of vice president in charge of the industrial section of Shanghai. In fact, he felt so confident in his future that it was not long before he invited Emily Duthie (Amy as she was known) to come to Shanghai to marry him.

On August 8th, 1929, twenty-four year old Amy sailed on the P & O steamship *Mantua*, following the same route as Sam and Eric before her. This was a brave and daring thing for a young lady to do all alone in those days, and it says a lot for her character. Other passengers on her ship consisted of 37 couples, 128 single men and 41 single women, so she may not have been the only bride on her way to be married. She made some good friends whose company she enjoyed again once she had settled into her new life in Shanghai.

My parents, Eric and Amy, were married on September 18th, 1929. They had a civil ceremony at the British Consulate General, officiated by Frank Arnold Wallis and witnessed by Sam and a friend, Ester Howard. This was followed by a wedding celebration at their new home at 80 Tifeng Road, solemnized by the Rev. Ernest F. B. Smith. Eric and Sam wore white linen suits and Amy had a beautiful, short, silk chiffon dress, decorated with lace and pearls, and a long veil held in place with orange blossom. She carried a large bouquet of orchids. There was a matron of honour and two bridesmaids, all in gossamer silk chiffon dresses with tiered skirts. They were an elegant group of people, preserved on surviving photographs, and it was obviously a very happy event. I, Eric Duncan Colterjohn, was born almost a year later on August 6th, 1930, at the Country Hospital in Shanghai.

Sam returned to Scotland on long leave in early 1930. He travelled across the Pacific on the SS *Empress of Canada*, arriving in Vancouver on May 30th. From there, he made his way across Canada, probably visiting his brother, Bill en route. He then sailed from Montreal on the *SS Duchess of Bedford* and arrived in Liverpool, England on June 14th. As Eric and Amy settled down to family life in Shanghai, Sam was courting Mary

Jacks Tait, also from Bo'ness. He finally returned to Shanghai, with Mary as his wife, on the P & O Steamship *Macedonia,* leaving London on September 19ᵗʰ. The bachelors had finally succumbed to a domestic life and were ready to settle down.

❀   ❀   ❀   ❀   ❀

One of the first, and most important, things all Westerners have to learn when they arrive in Asia is about *face.* I am taking a liberty in even attempting to define it, but feel that it is important enough to try. It is a combination of honour, pride, integrity, diligence and sense of self-worth, yet none of these things. It is a belief in the very essence of oneself, totally illusive but essential to all Chinese. It has no bearing on social rank, occupation or wealth, can be closely linked to the chain of command, but is not part of it. In a country of hundreds of millions of people crowded into cramped living and working conditions, face is what enables them to walk with their heads held high and provides the strength to survive in adversity. Occidentals frequently give unintended offense by not understanding the rules. It is very important to *save face* for all parties concerned, while negotiating a business deal or just talking to a friend. Even the most modest of housewives, like Amy and Mary, had to know how to direct and reprimand their domestic staff without causing them loss of face. Many years later, my wife and I would have hands-on experience of this when we lived in Malaya.

Although most societies have their order of things, hierarchy, and observance of rank, this goes far beyond the Western understanding of protocol, especially in Shanghai of the 1930s. In this city of a million shades of grey on an infinite number of levels, observing the correct chain of command was of paramount importance. One had to know exactly what one could say and to whom, when dealing with the Chinese of any social level. In business, your own rank, equated by business position, dictated who you could deal with within you own company and when dealing with others. In the big banks and businesses, there was a Chinese hierarchy similar to that of the foreigners with a strict protocol regarding communication between the two. A foreign executive would only give orders or directions to local staff through the Chinese *comprador* or manager. If anyone was bypassed in this complicated process they would lose face, often with serious consequences.

This process had to be observed in all dealings with the Chinese in Shanghai. If you wished to reserve a table at a special restaurant, you only discussed this with the maître d'. In a household with several members of staff, you only gave directions to the *number one boy*. If it was important for you to address a matter directly with the cook, chauffeur or the baby amah, you requested that *Number One* bring the other servant to you. Each employee knew his own place and was responsible for those under him or her. In this way, each person did his best to perform what was expected of him. If he failed in this, not only he, but the whole chain would lose face. In many ways, this was similar to the system below stairs in the large country homes of Victorian England, but with even more subtleties and on a much larger scale. Both Sam and Eric would say in later years that they preferred to work with the Chinese than any other race, and this was largely due to the system of face.

Another system that foreigners had to be aware of in the 1930s, although it was not so subtle or complicated, was that of *percentage*. Everyone from rickshaw pullers to taxi drivers, from sing-song girls to cabaret dancers, from construction coolies to factory workers paid a percentage to someone. This was either for finding them a job or for hiring them. It might not have been fair, but it was just the way it was. Just as pimps took their percentage from prostitutes, beggars paid a percentage for their corner of the pavement. I remember clearly seeing a couple of beggars getting out of a Rolls Royce when I was a child. My father told me that the car belonged to the king of the beggars and they were being dropped off at work. The king himself was very wealthy and held a position in society.

Protection was another racket that everyone observed to some extent or another. In the West, one bought insurance and, in the event that you were robbed or injured, the company compensated you for your loss or inconvenience. In the East, one bought protection against the problem happening in the first place. Obviously, neither system was infallible, but it is interesting to reflect on the differences in the Oriental and Occidental minds in this as in so many other things. This was Shanghai and how it worked. The Colterjohns, like all other foreigners who lived there, had to learn to play by the rules.

THE RISE OF JAPANESE AGGRESSION

1929 - 1932

As the United States of America was staggering under the weight of the Great Depression and the Wall Street Crash of October 1929, Shanghai was reaching the heights of its financial and business prosperity and social opulence. There were many reasons for this, but the huge manufacturing base, which was increasing all the time, was the most significant. The port was now the fifth largest in the world and it imported about 50 percent of China's imports and handled 30 percent of its exports, each in its own way contributing towards Shanghai's huge success. The establishment of the Nationalist government in Nanking brought a sense of stability to the country, and a stronger Chinese administration in Shanghai gave the Chinese Shanghainese a sense of identity. The Nationalist government felt there was no safer place in all of China than the big Chinese banks on the Bund in Shanghai, and deposited the national silver reserves there. The value of downtown real estate tripled in five years, making it some of the highest-priced land in the world, and the international banks attracted investments from depression-torn America and Europe, where banks were collapsing one after the other.

In 1930, the Shanghai Municipal Council's voters finally awarded five Chinese seats on the council. As a result, the British lost their overall majority but they realised that the time had come to co-operate more closely with the powerful Chinese bankers and businessmen or they could lose everything.

The Japanese response to this was to demand a further seat to add to the 14 that they already had. They also demanded the right to provide a Japanese security force to protect their interests in their community in Hongkew, known as Little Tokyo. This was approved by the SMC and it was made an auxiliary branch to the Shanghai Municipal Police. After the First World War, there had been about 20,000 Japanese living in the greater Shanghai area, but by 1930 this number had grown so fast that they were now the largest foreign group, even surpassing the British. Investments from Japan, as well as people, were flooding into Shanghai and by this time they owned the largest number of factories of any foreign nation. They were a very tight-knit group and, for the most part, stayed in their own community with very little social contact with the rest of the city. Other foreigners sometimes ate at the sukiyaki houses, but otherwise never entered Little Tokyo.

Shanghai was not the only area where the Japanese were increasing their numbers. They had been infiltrating Manchuria gradually for several years, and had built a large community there. On September 18th, 1931 a small bomb exploded on a Japanese railway line near Mukden, the capital of Manchuria. It had almost certainly been put there by the Japanese, as this was typical of the way they operated. Throughout history, Japan used the same tactics of intentionally causing a small incident, which they then blamed on another party, as a means of causing confrontation. Even the famous naval battle with China in 1894, resulting in the Treaty of Shimonoseki, was started this way.

The Japanese immediately took over the province and annexed it as a puppet state of Japan, calling it the Republic of Manchukuo. The deposed Manchurian Emperor, Pu-Yi was installed as its titular head. The Manchurian warlord had appealed to Chiang Kai-Shek for help but was told not to resist. As the Manchurians could in no way compete with the Japanese army on their own, they surrendered with little resistance. For the next few years, the local population would live as second class citizens, restricted in every way of life including what they could eat, where they could work and which schools their children could attend.

The reaction in Shanghai to the Mukden Incident was a burst of intense patriotism, in which even the Westerners shared. There was an immediate embargo placed on all Japanese businesses and goods with huge penalties for disobeying them. This was so effective that numerous Japanese factories and businesses had to close down, and many families were repatriated to Japan. Japanese ships lay in the roads and at the docks unable to discharge their cargos, and goods spoiled in their godowns and warehouses.

Things reached a climax on January 18th, 1932 when a group of Japanese monks from a militant Buddhist sect provoked a Chinese crowd to violence, with one monk being killed and two more injured. Ten days later, an elite unit of Japanese marines attacked Chapei, the heart of the Chinese business and manufacturing sector of Shanghai, with the North Railway Station as their principal target. Appeals to Chiang Kai-shek to send re-enforcements were to no avail, but the valiant Chinese troops that were there managed to hold out for five weeks. At this point, planes flew in from Japanese cruisers anchored in the Whuangpoo River and chequer-bombed Chapei. The township was almost completely reduced to rubble and about 10,000 civilians were killed. Hundreds of thousands of refugees took sanction in the International Settlement, where temporary camps were set up for them in all the Chinese public buildings and wherever else they could find space. It was the first time this form of warfare had been demonstrated anywhere in the world, and would become the model for many more to come. The Shanghai press gave the attack extensive coverage worldwide, where it was received with horror. In response to international criticism, Japan eventually resigned from the League of Nations.

❀ ❀ ❀ ❀ ❀

A truce was negotiated on May 5th, with both sides agreeing that Shanghai would become a demilitarized zone, except for the garrisons. The Japanese had to remove all their troops from the city and the Chinese had to withdraw theirs to 30 miles outside the city limits. The Sino-Japanese war did not officially start for another five years, but Japan had lost face with the rest of Shanghai and would be feared and hated from then on. Under the Treaty of Shimonoseki, they still had the right to live and work there but, even in a city of dozens of nationalities, they became the outsiders.

The rest of the foreign community reeled with shock and horror. They were relatively safe within the International Settlement, as the attack was obviously directed at the Chinese community, but there was a strong possibility that a misdirected bomb could land in their midst. This, in fact, is exactly what happened some years later. It must have seemed incomprehensible that one of the foreign nations that shared the same privileges and extraterritorial rights under the Unequal Treaties as they did should be attacking Shanghai in this horrendous way. These Japanese were their neighbours. Eric supplied power to their factories in Hongkew, which was part of the International Settlement, and many foreigners ate sukiyaki in their restaurants. The Japanese had 15 seats on the Shanghai Municipal Council. However much the sanctions were hurting them, surely nothing could justify such a vicious attack on a country with which they were not officially at war.

The resilience of the Chinese community was amazing. They buried their dead and cleared away the rubble of what had been their thriving community of Chapei, now almost completely destroyed. In place of the dark alleys and over-crowded shacks, they built wide streets designed for motor traffic, a proud new civic centre, hospitals and schools. Apartment buildings with modern plumbing took over from the old shanty towns. Efficient shop-houses and office buildings gave a boost to reviving commerce. New factories with modern machinery revolutionized the Chinese industrial sector. Obviously, this did not happen overnight but the will was so great that they found the way, and all Shanghai was behind their efforts.

THE SOCIAL SCENE

1932 - 1936

Most of the foreigners who came to live and work in Shanghai were seeking adventure and fortune, so were not easily frightened away. Some were of the same stock that had built the British Empire in the previous century. Basically, this was a middle class society, at least for the British and most Europeans, and social status was defined by wealth and, to a lesser extent, by occupation and business rank. Those from aristocratic or landed families were usually the younger sons, who had a much better chance of finding a comfortable way of life in the colonies or in places like Shanghai, due to the primogenital rules of succession at home. Many others were refugees from countries that they could not return to, even if they wished. Others still, were black sheep, criminals or, for whatever reason, simply wished to be absent from their home country for a few years. So, once the crisis had settled, after the Japanese assault on Shanghai in January 1932, the Chinese community concentrated their efforts on rebuilding Chapei, and the foreigners dusted themselves off and went back to their lives as usual.

However, it must have been hard on the young wives like my mother and my aunt Mary. Sam and Mary's first child, Albert Ian was born on August 24th, 1931 so was only about five months old when the Japanese attacked the city. I was almost 18 months and full of energy. But the Colterjohns seemed to have accepted it as part of life in Shanghai and continued with their many activities. The two families had moved to more spacious accommodation at 108 Tifeng Road before little Ian was born, so both ladies were busy arranging their new homes. This was an English compound with large three-storey semi-detached houses built in pairs around a park, and there are several surviving photographs of these homes and the kids playing there. As servants were part of the Shanghai lifestyle, Amy and Mary enjoyed entertaining in this lovely setting.

The Long Bar of the Shanghai Club, and other places where men discussed business, would have been lively as they speculated on how serious the threat of further Japanese attacks were, but these things would never have been discussed in front of ladies. This was still an era where a man preferred his wife to be decorative, fun and witty but not too well informed or over-educated. Their job was to rule the household, manage the children and the servants, and to organize dinner parties and the family's social life. They would be bathed, dressed and available to entertain their husbands when they returned from work. How they spent the rest of the day was largely up to them.

Bridge and mah-jong parties were popular and they could read as long as the books were not too serious. It must have been very hard on those ladies blessed with a good brain and a desire to actually do something intelligent. By the 1930s, women were becoming better educated in Britain, Europe and America, but Shanghai, with excellent domestic help to free up the Westerners' time, was still a place where ladies were expected to be beautiful, a little silly and fun. Although most American women achieved the right to vote in principle in 1920, it was not until 1928 that all British women over the age of 21 finally won this right. Amy and Mary had not even had an opportunity to vote.

Another subject that was never discussed in front of the ladies was money, and they had little need to carry any. They had signing rights in all the clubs they frequented and in the big department stores. Cookie did all the marketing for food, and their contribution to meal planning usually ended after a short discussion with him each morning. The family chauffeur drove them wherever they wanted to go and, if they really needed some cash, they had to ask their husbands for it. When they went out to restaurants and entertainment in the evenings, they would always be accompanied by their husband or a suitable escort.

❀ ❀ ❀ ❀ ❀

This was the age of cocktails, the Charleston, flapper dresses, cloche hats and cigarettes on long ivory holders. Beads and fringes were on everything from skirts to lampshades. This huge multi-cultural city offered more forms of entertainment than any other city in the world at that time. One could eat the cuisine from a different country every night for a month, and follow that with a different club, show or cabaret. It is no wonder that Shanghai quickly became the favourite port of call for the cruise ships that started arriving in the late 1920s.

The most serious vices had been outlawed by both the Nationalist Party and the Shanghai Municipal Council by 1930. In Shanghai, this meant that opium dens, brothels and gaming houses of the lowest types went underground, while upper class casinos and expensive ladies-for-hire did better than ever, especially in the French Concession. With an extensive population of single men, both Chinese and foreign, there was a constant demand for female company at all levels. These ladies fell into two distinct categories: those who were specifically hired to provide sexual services as part of their job, and those who were allowed to use their own discretion. This made a big difference to what they could charge and to their future expectations.

The courtesans were at the top of the scale and were drawn from all nationalities. One house employed so many foreigners that it became known as *The American Girls*. The most skilled and successful courtesan could make enough money to own a large house with servants and would only be approached by a man with a written letter of introduction. A lengthy and expensive courtship would follow with no guarantee of ever reaching the lady's bed. Even an average girl, like those who provided escort services to visiting businessmen, could earn a good living. These courtesans often married well when they decided to retire. Some of the foreign ladies were already married but liked to make a little discreet money on the side while their husbands were away.

Further down the social scale came the sing-song girls and taxi-dance partners. These were mostly Chinese and were often young country girls who had recently arrived in the city to make their fortune or to find a husband. They performed in the tea-houses and dance halls and were not obliged to provide sexual favours. However, arrangements were often made privately for these. The prettiest and most talented had a good chance of finding a suitable husband or of becoming a concubine with a secure future. On the other side of the line, establishments ranged from high-class bordellos, patronized by the rich and discerning, to destitute streetwalkers. Every taste was catered for.

❈   ❈   ❈   ❈   ❈

By 1932, there were at least 48,000 foreigners living and working in Shanghai. These came from as many as 20 major nationalities, and many smaller groups from other countries. Some of them enjoyed extraterritorial privileges and all the advantages of being members of the Unequal Treaties, but many, like the White Russians and other refugees, did not. This, in itself, created big divisions within the community, especially economic and linguistic. The original settlers, in particular the British, French and Americans, were well established as the leaders, with seats on the Municipal Council, and gunboats anchored in the Whuangpoo River to guard their national interests. This all contributed to the segregation of the community into national enclaves, unlike most large European cities. They worked together where necessary, and played together, but usually in neutral territory like clubs and restaurants. By this time, there was also a large number of wealthy, upper and middle class Chinese, many of whom had been edu-

cated abroad, who could also be found mixing with the foreigners in the night clubs and cabarets. Private parties were
slowly starting to break down social barriers, but mostly
among the very rich or for business purposes.

By co-incidence, both Sam and Eric were British but worked
for American companies. This enabled them to enjoy the social
life of both cultures to a point. Years later, my parents would
talk about this and how they had had many more American
friends than most British residents. This gave them access to
both country clubs, with very different activities and atmos-
pheres. The British one was more formal, especially in the dining room, while we children were introduced to hot dogs,
hamburgers and chips as a special treat, in the Columbia
Country Club, which was American. Amy and Mary loved
swimming, tennis and dancing, all of which they were able to
do regularly, and many photographs have survived to support
this. Thirty years later, my mother still had a trunk of her favourite silk evening dresses, mostly in shift and flapper styles,
lovely ivory fans and other delightful trinkets.

❀   ❀   ❀   ❀   ❀

It was customary for most companies in the East to give their
employees six months leave, or furlough as it was called, every
five years. In April, 1933, my family left Shanghai for our first
leave and my parents must have felt ready for a break, after all
the horrendous events of the previous year. In spite of the hostile feelings toward the Japanese, they decided to visit Japan
en route home to Scotland. We eventually sailed from Yoko-
hama on the Japanese steamship *Terukuni Maru*, arriving in
London on May 3rd, Amy's birthday. After our life in Shanghai, this must have been something of a cultural shock, but we
were delighted to be united with my grandparents.

Almost exactly a year later, Sam, Mary and Ian also took off
on furlough, but sailed in the opposite direction on the Canadian Pacific steamship *Empress of Asia,* from Shanghai to
Vancouver. They crossed Canada by train to Quebec City,

where they sailed for Southampton on the *Empress of Australia*, arriving on May 19th, 1934. Both families followed much the same pattern while in Scotland. We usually rented a house in Edinburgh to use as a base, and then divided our time among the various relatives. My grandfather, Albert Colterjohn, and Mary's family were still living in Bo'ness, just a short drive from Edinburgh, but my mother's family was in Sandhaven, north of Aberdeen. I loved those trips to Sandhaven and the excitement of watching ships being built in the boatyard where my grandfather worked. The wildness of the North Sea was very much in my blood and I felt that all my life. On August 3, 1934, Sam and his family returned to Shanghai on the P. & O. Steamship *Rawalpindi*, so our two families were together again by September.

❀ ❀ ❀ ❀ ❀

The mid-1930s were one of the most exciting periods to be in Shanghai. The Cathay Hotel, in front of the Sassoon building, had opened its magnificent doors in 1929, bringing a whole new meaning to luxurious hospitality. This had two elevators and telephones in each room - unheard of before this. The rich and famous from all over the world could be found wining, dining and dancing there any day of the week. This was followed by the construction of several enormous new apartment buildings with every form of modern convenience, including room service from restaurants and beauty parlours on the street level. These quickly became the new rage for the wealthy, as the elite moved into the city centre from their suburban mansions, and the skyline of Shanghai changed with higher and more innovative buildings.

These modern trends did not really affect the Colterjohns, as we loved our homes in Tifeng Road. It was a protected compound and a convenient location for all that we liked to do. We were close to a big market and Ian and I enjoyed being taken there by our amahs. How we loved the smell of chicken and pork being roasted over charcoal burners. If we were really good, the amahs would buy us pieces of twisted dough, fried in deep fat and covered with sugar. This was the forerunner of the Western doughnut. The market was full of multi-coloured fruit and vegetables, exotic smells and all types of people imaginable, including beggars shaking their round cigarette tins and calling "No papa, no mama, no whiskey soda". These were the things that created life-long memories for Ian and me.

On Chinese feast days, weddings and all special occasions, fire-crackers would shatter the peace of the night and light up the sky to ward off the evil spirits. Sometimes there would be dragon dances, with several people inside the dragon costume, weaving their way in and out of the crowds and the traffic. These costumes were a work of art with huge jewelled heads and embroidered bodies that could be up to 12 or 15 feet long. They were passed down from generation to generation as prized possessions.

The long funeral processions were of special interest to the foreigners. Dozens of paid mourners dressed in white would lead the way with family members, protected by canopies, following. There would be at least one photograph of the deceased, and all his favourite worldly goods were reproduced in coloured paper, which was burned at the grave. The richer the deceased, the longer and more elaborate the procession, which could stretch for several blocks. Bands, flowers and a general air of celebration made these events fun to watch.

Our favourite recreational spot was the Race Club with its big variety of activities. The racetrack ran around the outside, leaving a big park in the middle for other sports like polo, cricket, baseball, tennis, lawn bowling and a nine hole golf course. It also had a big swimming pool and several restaurants. I especially loved visiting the stables to see the race horses. My father won the Coronation Cup there, donated to the golf club to celebrate the crowning of King George VI and Queen Elizabeth, and displayed this proudly for the rest of his life.

Our family enjoyed the sailing regattas held on the Whuangpoo at Kiangwan, to the north of Shanghai, although we never owned our own boat. Luckily, several of our friends did, so it became a favourite weekend pastime. Sometimes, we would sail upstream, but had to be careful not to go beyond the patrolled area, because of the danger of encountering bandits and pirates. Jessfield Park was another common weekend destination, situated a few miles out of the city. For longer trips, we went to the seaside at Tsingtao and Iltis-Huk, with their beautiful sandy beaches. We rented bungalows and relaxed away from the hustle and bustle of Shanghai. Many photos have survived of these happy holidays. These were halcyon days and we lived them to the full.

❀ ❀ ❀ ❀ ❀

On March 13th, 1935 my brother Colin Duthie was born. The family always said that I was a true Colterjohn; small but athletic, fair curly hair and blue eyes, but the new baby had dark hair and brown eyes like our mother. She absolutely adored him and, when he died about 20 years later in an accident, she never came to terms with it. In September of that year, I was enrolled at the Cathedral School, of the Holy Trinity Anglican Cathedral. I loved it there and was enormously proud of my new blazer, although I never made the choir, of which the school was quite famous.

The following year, on February 27th, 1936 Mary presented Ian with a baby sister, Janet Maureen, and in September Ian joined me at the Cathedral School. We were the only Scottish Colterjohns of that generation, as neither Jean nor Bill would have children. We were all born in Shanghai, but were to travel extensively around the world throughout our lives and finally settle elsewhere.

THE LONG MARCH
1934 - 1936

Shanghai had long been a hotbed of international intrigue but, after the Shanghai Massacre, there were more snoops and spies per square mile than anywhere else on earth. Most Communists who had survived the slaughter had left Shanghai, except for the Central Executive Committee. They had to go deep underground and received support from the Comintern and other Communist groups from around the world. It soon became the Communist headquarters of Asia with the establishment of a Far Eastern Bureau. Many people wore two caps and one could never be sure who was affiliated with whom.

In early 1931, the Nationalist government in Nanking passed a law making it a crime to oppose or criticize the government in any way. All Communists, real or alleged, were punished by death or life imprisonment. Chiang Kai-shek's witch-hunt intensified, with the help of the Shanghai Municipal Council Police and the French Gendarmerie, and it eventually paid off with the arrest of the head of the Shanghai Bureau. This exposed the full extent of the network and the Bureau was completely dismantled and closed down in 1934.

Those Communists who had managed to escape from Shanghai in 1927, had regrouped in the mountains of Jiangxi, south China, in an area called Jinggangshan. This covered about 1200 square miles in one of the most remote areas of the country. There were no roads, just small towns and villages, serviced by dirt tracks, and the local peasants were very poor. The Communists had to come to terms with several unfriendly warlords but, having done this, were able to relax for a few months and recruit new troops. In 1929, as their numbers increased, and local warlords became more possessive of their territory, they outgrew the resources of the area and moved the Red Army to South Jiangxi and the western part of Fujian Province, where they set up the new Central Soviet Area. By November 1932, they had declared this the Soviet Republic of China, with Ruijin as its capital and with a population of about three million. They still took direction from the Central Committee in Shanghai at this point, but many of their Chinese leaders were leaving Shanghai to join the main group, and they gradually took over command breaking with the Far Eastern Bureau, even before its collapse.

The Communists were scrupulous in their dealings with the local peasants. The troops were well behaved and all food, materials and lodgings were paid for at a fair price. This soon won them the trust and respect of the local people, and no other part of China would enrol so many of their sons in the Red Army or, eventually, lose so many in the struggle ahead. Recruits and their families were given many incentives to join, including gifts of salt, fuel, cotton goods and matches, and a pledge of security to the families should their sons be killed. They also promised everyone would own land when the Communists came to power, at the expense of the landlords, of course. In the years to come, they did their best to honour these pledges and settle all unpaid debts. This was in huge contrast to the unruly behaviour of the Nationalist Army.

❋   ❋   ❋   ❋   ❋

Chiang Kai-shek had employed a German as a tactical advisor, when the Soviet Russian Councillors had gone home, and he directed the Nationalist army of about 700,000 men to completely surround the Communist-held area. They defeated the

Red Army in battle after battle. Slowly, they tightened the noose, and reduced the supplies to the Communists, confident that their success was inevitable. This probably made them over-confident and bored, with the many months of waiting as, when the break-out came, they missed it.

On the night of October 16, 1934 some 86,000 men and women of the Red Army quietly slipped out of the noose and crossed the Yudu River, where engineers had made pontoons to ferry the heavy loads to the other side. The river was low enough for much of the army to walk across in the moonlight. They took all their worldly possessions including a mass of equipment like printing presses, X-ray machines, and the paraphernalia of warfare. They had all the party records, chests of silver dollars, gold bars, radio equipment and supplies to feed this huge army. Each man had to carry his own essentials, bed-roll and food for a number of days and porters, who came and went as they passed out of their home area, were hired to carry the rest.

This was an enormous group, covering 60 miles from end to end, with the fighting units at the front and bringing up the rear. In between, were the supply trains, non-combatants, women, children and the injured. The leaders, Mao Tse-tung, Chou Enlai, Bo Gu, and Zhu De, to mention just a few, had horses to ride up and down the column. There was also a German advisor, known as Otto Braun (among other aliases) who was the planner of this great exodus. They marched by night and hid by day but, even then, it is almost unbelievable that it took several days for the Nationalist Army to realize that the Red Army had escaped them. Inevitably, a large group had been left behind, being too old, too young or too sick to make the march, with an army left to protect them. When Chiang Kai-shek discovered what had happened, his fury held no bounds and he sent his troops in to annihilate those left behind.

❁   ❁   ❁   ❁   ❁

No one knew where they were going or how long it would take to get there. In fact, it took almost exactly a year, and they arrived in Yan'an, North Shaanxi Province, on October 19th, 1935. Of the original 86,000 who had crossed the Yudu River in south China, only about 4,000 lived to reach their destination. They had marched on foot for about 6,000 miles across arid desert, quick-sand and bottomless bogs. They had crossed over about 20 major rivers and climbed through mountain ranges thought to be impenetrable, all without roads. They had frozen, starved, and struggled on against all odds, fighting both the Nationalist Army and unfriendly warlords as they went. They were constantly sought out by Chiang's planes and strafed and bombed, but still they struggled on. They even went through periods where the leadership of the group was challenged. Most importantly, they had won the hearts and minds of millions of peasants in areas of China so remote that they had never seen a stranger and where they did not even have a common language. Everywhere the Red Army went, they behaved kindly to the locals, paid for what they took and made converts to the Communist ideals. They promised free land for all and personal dignity. Some of these promises they were able to keep, others not, but their intentions were honest and honourable at the time they were made.

❀ ❀ ❀ ❀ ❀

Part of the huge army had been separated from the main column and it would be about another year before all these parts became united on October 2nd, 1936. Finally, in December of that year, they established their new base in Bao'an, North Shaanxi. Mao Tse-tung had declared war against the Japanese, even before they left Jiangxi, and it was now time to establish this as their new priority. Every attempt to make peace with Chiang and the Kuomintang in a common effort to halt the Japanese advance was rebuffed. As a desperate measure, two warlords friendly to the Nationalists, kidnapped Chiang, in what history calls the Xi'an Incident. Even the

members of Chiang's own party were disillusioned with his total obsession with persecuting the Communists to the exclusion of all else. Chiang was eventually released on Christmas
Day, on the condition that he formed a coalition with the Red
Army to stop the advance of the Japanese.

This was an uneasy alliance and came too little and too late.
All those years when Chiang had turned his back on Manchuria, and even the attack on Shanghai, to pursue the Red Army,
the Japanese had been quietly expanding their forces and
equipment in Manchukuo and north China. By now, they had
the most highly-trained army of that time, equipped with
modern means of warfare, and had had several peaceful years
to prepare for a complete takeover of China.

THE DREAM SHATTERS
1937

On July 7th, 1937 the Japanese army created an incident at the Marco Polo Bridge near Peking over a missing soldier. He was later found in a brothel, but this did not stop the army from capturing the bridge. As this was in a very strategic location, it quickly escalated into full-scale war. By the end of July, the cities of Peking and Tientsin, and the areas surrounding them, had fallen under Japanese occupation, giving them control of Manchuria and a large area of northern China. Although war had not actually been declared, it is generally accepted that this was the official start of the second Sino-Japanese war, eventually leading into the Second World War in Asia.

Chiang Kai-shek could no longer ignore the situation, but was ill-equipped and far from ready to do battle with the Japanese forces, which were superior by land, sea and air. The Nationalists had recently formed a loose coalition with the Communists and on August 2nd, Chiang legalized the Red Army and they joined forces under the banner of the United Front. However, many of the experienced soldiers from both groups had gone back to their villages, disillusioned and exhausted after the Long March ended. The army that was left was largely made up of young, inexperienced recruits, poorly disciplined and badly trained by weary and corrupt officers. Morale was low and their tools of war were outdated or non-existent. In some areas, they were also outnumbered by the Japanese, who were able to bring in fresh reinforcements easily and quickly by ship from Japan.

Chiang realised the weakness of his situation and signed a non-aggression pact with the USSR on August 1st. Russia, who preferred the Japanese to be at war with China, rather than attacking their own borders, came to China's aid with money, aeroplanes and ammunition. Chiang felt that his best hope was to concentrate his forces in the Yangtze Valley, where he was familiar with the terrain, and ordered his troops to Shanghai. Mistakenly, he also hoped that the threat to the city would bring support from the foreign warships there. The Japanese responded to this by doubling the size of their army camped around Shanghai and adding many more ships to their fleet anchored in the Whangpoo River. In fact, they brazenly moved them upriver with their flagship *Idzumo* right in front of the Bund.

❀ ❀ ❀ ❀ ❀

As children, we found this very exciting, and I remember celebrating my seventh birthday on August 6th by playing "Chinks and Japs" with my friends - the Eastern version of cowboys and Indians. Everyone wanted to be a Jap, so that they could pretend to fire the big guns on the warships in the river. The Japs were the bad guys, but only nominally so, because our parents kept talking about the imminent Japanese invasion. This was really quite confusing to us. Shanghai was full of Japanese residents, and my father had many Japanese clients who I knew he liked and respected. One of my favourite treats was to go to the Sukiyaki restaurants in Little Tokyo, and it was hard to accept that these people were suddenly our enemies.

However, we soon discovered what real war was all about. A week later, in the evening of August 13th, sporadic firing began. This caused immediate panic and hundreds of thousands of Chinese flooded into the International Settlement and the French Concession for protection. Chinese and foreigners worked together to convert every possible building from cinemas and dance halls to sports stadiums and racecourses into shelters. About 350,000 Chinese managed to leave Shanghai in time to return to their villages, or to join either the Nationalist or Communist armies. The Chinese community had barely finished rebuilding Chapei and their worst fears were being realised all over again.

The following day, Chinese aeroplanes tried to attack the *Idzumo* and the warships around her. She trained her big guns on them hitting several planes, whose pilots panicked and discharged their bombs over the city instead of their targets. One fell through the roof of the Palace Hotel and another in front of the Cathay Hotel next door, at the intersection of the Bund and Nanking Road. As the area was packed with both residents and refugees, the number of people killed and injured was enormous and included many foreigners. Falling glass from the high buildings probably injured as many as the actual bomb blasts. Two more bombs landed in the middle of a large group of refugees being served with free food at the corner of Eduoard VII and Thibet roads near the Racecourse. The death toll was even higher there. Ironically, the worst day of the siege of Shanghai with over 3,000 people killed in a few hours, was caused by Chinese planes by accident, and not by the Japanese.

❀ ❀ ❀ ❀ ❀

Three months of intense fighting followed and the Chinese army, ill-equipped as they were, fought incredibly bravely but took enormous losses. Chiang Kai-shek had given orders that they were to hold Shanghai to the last man, to buy time to evacuate the Nationalist Government from Nanking to Hankow (Wuhan), knowing that Nanking would be attacked next. Finally, reduced to a third of their original number, the Chinese army retreated, setting fire to what was left of Chapei as they went. This provided a temporary barrier between them and the advancing Japanese, but Chapei and much of Hongkew and Pootung were once again devastated.

By mid-November the Chinese parts of Shanghai had surrendered. On December 3rd· the Japanese army organised a
victory parade down the Nanking Road and then moved off to
ravage the countryside on their way to Nanking. The city was
filled with the smoke of burning corpses and dust from the
rubble, reminiscent of only five years earlier. Once more,
Shanghai had to clear away the devastation of war and rebuild.
However, unlike the 1932 attack, the Japanese were now in
control of what was left of the Chinese sections of the city. The
International Settlement and the French Concession were
packed with hundreds of thousands of refugees who had to be
housed and fed. The Chinese industrial sectors had been completely destroyed and a large percentage of the foreign-owned
businesses had been closed. The farmland around the city had
been trampled by the attacking armies. They had destroyed the
crops and killed the livestock. Most of these refugees were not
only without homes and food but also without employment.

❀　❀　❀　❀　❀

Throughout the horrors of August 13th and 14th, the warships
belonging to the Western nations anchored in the Whangpoo
were unable to come to the city's aid without the risk of initiat-
ing a world conflict. However, they could rescue their nationals, and this they started to do immediately, evacuating about
5,000 foreigners alone. This time, Uncle Sam and my father
insisted that we children leave with our mothers at once, and
so we were taken to Hong Kong in a British gunboat, an experience that Ian and I would never forget. The first evacuations
would probably have been women and children, but it is possible that my Uncle Sam accompanied us, as he no longer had a
job to go to. My father certainly stayed behind to continue
working at the Shanghai Power Company and to look after our
homes in Tifeng Road. He joined us for short holidays from
time to time, but his job was too essential to spend much time
away from it.

Many foreign-owned businesses and factories had been closing down their operations for some weeks, in anticipation of hostilities, so it is probable that Anderson, Meyers & Co. closed the factory before the siege of Shanghai and relocated the equipment to other plants in safer locations. When Vilhelm Meyer died in 1934, the surviving partner, General Electric, took over the company, which then became the Chinese headquarters of GE. They had continually expanded over the years that Sam worked there and, by this time, had nine plants in China, manufacturing an enormous diversification of products. I remember that Uncle Sam stayed with us in Hong Kong after the evacuation, so he may even have been offered a job with the Hong Kong GE plant while he was there.

❀ ❀ ❀ ❀ ❀

We lived in Hong Kong for the next few months, which made an interesting change for us but, even in Hong Kong, things were not dull. Early in the morning of September 2nd, the island was hit by one of the worst typhoons in its history, killing or injuring more than 11,000 people; about one per cent of the total population. At that time, Hong Kong harbour was the seventh busiest port in the world. A cutting from a local newspaper, which has survived all these years, described it as follows:

Developing in the western Pacific Ocean, it moved in a west-northwest direction at the rate of about 32 km/h and passed 8 km to the south of the island before it made landfall on mainland China. As the typhoon passed, winds of up to 240 km/h were recorded in Hong Kong. Heavy rain fell, reaching 5.46 cm per hour. The most severe impact from the typhoon was a 9.1 m tidal wave that was pushed through the narrow Tolo Channel, located in the northeast area of Hong Kong. It swamped the low-lying villages of Taipo and Shatin, causing great damage and loss of life. The typhoon's winds were so strong that instruments at the Hong Kong Observatory, capable of registering winds up to 201 km/h, broke down.

During the height of the typhoon, the sea level in the harbor rose about 1.8 m (about 6 ft.) above the predicted level of the high tide. Many ships in the harbor, and even more at sea, were destroyed. At least 18 ocean liners and other large vessels were ripped from their moorings and careened across the harbor smashing into each other, eventually sinking or being carried ashore. Two cruise ships were actually swept up onto the pier, one of them colliding with a building. Thousands of fishing boats, junks, sampans, ferries and houseboats broke up and sank. Had it not been for the narrowness of Lyemoon Pass, the eastern entrance to Hong Kong Harbor, the surge could have been far worse.

My family was safe and unharmed. We were renting a two-story house part-way up the mountain, so were well away from the ferocious waves and the flooding. We woke up in the middle of the night from the noise of the wind and rain lashing the building. Trees were being torn up by their roots and flew past our windows with other items like deck chairs, umbrellas and anything else that was not tied down. Our parents took us downstairs with our pillows and quilts and we spent the rest of the night under the dining room table hugging the frightened dog. When daylight came, we could not believe our eyes and went downtown to see all the damage. The sight of the debris and all sizes of boats and ships scattered around the shoreline, even in the city streets, was beyond our wildest imagination. We wondered if there was anywhere safe left in the world. We had escaped from the Japanese in Shanghai only to be assaulted by nature in Hong Kong.

THE RAPE OF NANKING

1937 - 1938

W hat followed the battle of Shanghai is such a blot on mankind that it is almost beyond description. It has frequently been called the single worst act of premeditated savagery and mass murder of the entire Second World War, yet it has been almost forgotten by subsequent generations. To omit it in a story of this kind would be to do a grave injustice to the Chinese.

Chiang Kai-shek knew that they could not hold Nanking indefinitely so, in October 1937, started to evacuate the government to Hankow (Wuhan) and to establish new military headquarters there. This was further west into the interior of China on the Yangtze River, so they were able to use boats to take everything they could transport in the time available. This included factories that could be disbanded and transported. They not only took the machinery of government, but many of the riches and antiquities of the city for safekeeping. About half the population, including anyone who could afford to leave, left. They also took most of the food supplies, barely leaving enough for those 300,000 people remaining. As refugees poured in from the countryside, this number quickly doubled, leaving a critical food shortage, even before the siege started.

On December 7th, 1937 Chiang Kai-shek and his wife left Shanghai by air for Hankow. Two days later, international diplomats, journalists and some wealthy Chinese went aboard the US gunboat *Panay* and dropped anchor in the Yangtze, with the USA flag flying prominently. With the Japanese army almost on their doorstep, Chiang changed his mind about defending Nanking and ordered the army generals to abandon the city and to move their troops to Hankow. Unfortunately, the communications equipment had already been removed, so great confusion followed. The higher-ranking officers left their commands with their subordinates and hurriedly left Nanking by boat. Some commanders managed to lead their troops out of the city, hoping to head west ahead of the army. Others realised that there was no time, so took refuge within the city walls. The result was total chaos with no plan for the defence of the city and little communication between the Chinese army units.

Nanking was one China's most ancient and revered cities and had served as the national capital on many occasions. Although the city had long since spread outside the huge walls, they were still standing strong and the many gates were largely intact. It was embraced in a large curve of the Yangtze River, to the north and west, which normally provided some protection, but this time it worked against them. On December 9th, the Japanese army advanced from the southeast cutting off the retreating Chinese army, and slaughtered them all. The following day, a massive bombardment of the city started by land and by air. They even bombed and sank the *Panay*, strafing the survivors as they hid in the rushes along the banks of the river. After a very violent siege lasting four days, the remaining Chinese soldiers surrendered, and Nanking fell to the Japanese on December 13th, 1937.

❀   ❀   ❀   ❀   ❀

The Japanese had bragged that they could capture the whole of China in three months, so were shocked at the resilience and bravery of the Chinese army that had defended Shanghai for so long. Their casualties had been much higher than expected and morale was poor. Although they had captured the Chinese parts of Shanghai, the real treasures, the International Settlement and the French Concession, were still out of their grasp.

This made it a somewhat empty victory. To raise the spirits of their troops, officers gave orders to loot, burn and kill everyone in the towns and villages that they passed on the way to Nanking. They even encouraged a killing competition with prizes for the first to kill a hundred people. This was not done secretly. The score was published in the Tokyo newspapers to raise public morale.

This was the mood of the Japanese army as they arrived at Nanking. History has offered many excuses of false orders being issued, due to the illness of the commander-in-chief, and of the frustration of finding nothing worth fighting for when they did capture the city. However, nothing can excuse what followed. Once the Chinese surrendered, the Japanese soldiers tortured, raped and murdered an estimated 300,000 people with premeditated and unimaginable cruelty.

The figures would have been much higher, had not a group of heroic foreigners created an international safety zone to protect as many people as they could, although this was constantly violated by the Japanese. The stories of their selfless bravery are the only redeeming parts of this horrific event. The foreigners sent word of the massacre to the outside world and kept meticulous diaries, which were eventually made public. The story was published on the front pages of American and European newspapers, but most of their readers could not conceive that such tales could be true.

After murdering virtually the whole population, who were not being protected in the international safety zone, and burning down about one third of the city, the carnage came to an end in early February, 1938. The whole campaign had taken just over six weeks. The Japanese made Nanking their new base, from which to administer the parts of China already captured, and to launch attacks on the cities in the interior.

❀ ❀ ❀ ❀ ❀

In 1945, the American Air Force dropped two atomic bombs on Japan, killing fewer people than the Japanese had butchered in the Rape of Nanking. Under the terms of the surrender, Emperor Hirohito was granted immunity for himself and all the Imperial family from investigation during the subsequent war crimes trials. They never had to face a moral accounting.

A Parting of the Ways

1937 – 1939

This time, the foreign community in Shanghai knew the situation was serious and that doing business with the Japanese breathing down their necks would be difficult, if not impossible. The stories of Japanese atrocities in Nanking finally made them realise that the escalating Sino-Japanese war was something they could no longer ignore. The national silver and gold deposits had been removed to the safety of Hong Kong, and ships diverted to other ports. Many wealthy Chinese had been moving their investments to Hong Kong, the USA and other safer havens for several years, and now decided to follow their money.

For many foreigners, this was the time to re-evaluate their situation, especially those with young families. By the end of 1937, there was much speculation about another world war in Europe so, for some, continuing to live in Shanghai seemed to be the lesser of two evils. Others like the White Russian and Jewish refugees had few options. However, there was a large group who felt it was time to leave; Sam was one of these, especially as he no longer had a job to return to in Shanghai. On October 15th, Sam, Mary, Ian, and Maureen left Hong Kong on the *SS Empress of Asia* arriving in Victoria, BC, on November 1st. From there, they crossed Canada by train and sailed back to Scotland. Their Shanghai days were over.

My father, Eric, decided that he had a responsibility to stay, so my mother, Colin and I moved back from Hong Kong to our home in Tifeng Road in early February, 1938. The British Consul was advising British nationals to stand firm and protect their interests, especially those employed in essential services. My father fell into this category, which really left him little choice. They were reminded that Britain was not at war with Japan and that they had a legal right to continue to live and work in the treaty ports, especially Shanghai. The general feeling seems to have been that the Japanese had no reason to challenge these rights, as they already had the same privileges themselves, and that a *live and let live* policy would develop. After living in Shanghai for ten years, my family, like so many of the other foreign residents, felt that this was their home.

The social life in the international parts of the city was recovering and the cinemas, amusement houses, dance halls and other forms of entertainment had never been busier. The atmosphere of Shanghai was still frenetic but had somehow lost its spontaneous gaiety. Many old friends had left and their homes stood empty or were taken over by Chinese. The International Settlement and the French Concession were still full of Chinese refugees, and would be for some time to come, as they slowly tried to rebuild their lives in areas now under Japanese control. The halcyon days of this fun-loving city were over.

❀   ❀   ❀   ❀   ❀

In January, 1938, Japan formally declared war on China and announced that she no longer recognised the Nationalist Government. The Chinese ambassador to Japan was recalled and, from then on, hostilities increased. The foreigners in Shanghai knew very little or nothing about what was happening in the Chinese war with Japan. The press was only allowed to print reports of Chinese victories and successes, so the population away from the war zones was lulled into a false sense of security. The foreign countries represented in Shanghai were not at war with Japan, but their way of life was being seriously threatened. The Japanese were not just the enemy without, but very much part of their community. Although their immediate target was the Chinese sections of the city, the Japanese living there were slowly taking control of the International Settlement through domination of the municipal council and the police force.

They also developed an underground organisation dedicated to increasing vice and demoralizing the community. This was a more insidious form of aggression, but proved very effective and threatened everyone living in Shanghai, Chinese or foreign. However, the most frightening development was the campaign of terror instigated by the Japanese Kempei Tei (Secret Service) against Chinese patriots, at their headquarters at 76 Jessfield Road. Suddenly the whole city was full of subversive activity and no one knew whom they could trust. Intimidation of the press was the next threat and the bombing of newspaper offices, both Chinese and foreign, became frequent events.

Surprisingly, the port of Shanghai was still wide open to all who sought sanctuary there, with no questions asked or the requirement of visas and other documentation. Throughout 1938 and early 1939, as the city continued to rebuild, about 20,000 Jewish refugees from the increasing Nazi threat in Germany and central Europe flocked there. In fact, Shanghai was one of the very few places in the world that welcomed them, and the established Jewish community did their best to help. Most were destitute by the time they arrived, regardless of their original social status or wealth, and started their new lives in squalid poverty in the poorer parts of Hongkew, many in bombed-out buildings. However, they brought with them sharp minds and many professions and skills, which they were able to use to start new lives. Most of them gradually merged with the melee of other foreigners and found their niche, but it was a long, hard struggle.

⊛　⊛　⊛　⊛　⊛

In the spring of 1939, we were due for furlough. My parents must have planned this with much uncertainty and an open mind, as they took the precaution of shipping most of our valuable possessions back to Scotland before they left. This proved to be a wise decision as many of these beautiful Chinese artifacts are still being appreciated by subsequent generations. We sailed back to Scotland on the Norddeutscher Lloyd Line *SS Potsdam,* stopping in Sumatra and finally disembarking in Naples. We then proceeded by train across Europe, visiting Switzerland and Paris on the way. We rented a house in Edinburgh, as usual, and I, now eight years old, was enrolled at George Watson's Boys College for the coming term.

Sam and Mary had been living in Scotland for almost two years by then and our two families spent much time together catching up on all the news. War in Europe was now a certainty. The question was, what were the brothers were going to do about this. They had to decide whether to stay in Britain, enlist in one of the armed forces and fight in Europe or to return abroad where they could use their skills in other ways. They were no longer young men and Sam had been in the army in the Great War. Eric decided to go to the USA to visit the head office of the Shanghai Power Company and, on April 15th, sailed from Southampton to New York on the Cunard White Star Line *SS Queen Mary*. Whatever transpired there, it resulted in his decision to return to his job in Shanghai. On August 25th, my mother, Colin and I followed on the P & O *SS Viceroy of India*. War in Europe was declared on September 1st, 1939 while we were en route. We only just got out in time.

Sam, who had missed the life of Shanghai badly, as had Mary, decided to accept an appointment in Calcutta with the Indian General Electric Company. Two years later, he and his family moved to Jabalpur, Central India where Sam worked as manager of a gun carriage factory.

❀ ❀ ❀ ❀ ❀

Back in Shanghai, my parents decided that I should transfer from the Cathedral School to the Anglo-American School, where they felt I would get a better education. After the 1937

Japanese attack on Shanghai, the U.S. government had formally advised all American women and children to evacuate China. Although many did not comply with this, the foreign schools lost a lot of their pupils and many good teachers. Things were changing rapidly. Foreigners had always constricted their social life mostly to their own nationals, but now these groups became tighter than ever. A strong sense of caution prevailed and no-one could be trusted.

The sad news eventually reached us that grandfather Albert Colterjohn had died on October 14th, and we were very glad that we had spent some happy times with him so recently. Luckily, Uncle Sam and his family were still in Scotland and so were there to support my Aunt Jean. She would soon be the only Colterjohn left living there. Ian remembers that the funeral was on the first day that the Germans tried to bomb the Forth Bridge. This was on October 16th, 1939 and was, in fact, the first German air raid on Britain. The primary target was the huge naval docks at Rosyth near Edinburgh, with many of Britain's finest warships anchored there. The defences of the base were excellent, no-one was killed and very little damage was inflicted. The first enemy aircraft shot down in Britain in World War II, was in that raid.

❁ ❁ ❁ ❁ ❁

In August 1939, Soviet Russia and Germany signed a non-aggression pact, removing any hope of Russia's continued assistance to China. On June 10th, 1940 the Italians joined the war on the side of Germany. On June 22nd, France capitulated to the Germans and signed an armistice. The French government retreated to Vichy and remained officially neutral, but in fact pro-Axis, for the duration. The French Concession in Shanghai was now under the Vichy administration. Britain and other European countries were too involved in their own problems to be concerned with helping China. On September 27th, Germany, Italy and Japan signed the Tripartite Pact, creating the Axis Alliance. The significance of this was not lost on the

Shanghailanders, and many of the remaining women and children were evacuated, but not my family, who remained for almost another two years.

In September 1940, the Japanese invaded French Indochina, later known as Vietnam, Laos and Cambodia. Initially, this was to prevent the Chinese importation of arms and fuel by rail across that border. As Indochina was now ruled by Vichy France, who was an Axis sympathizer, the Japanese had hoped to negotiate an agreement with them to shut the border with China, and to supply Japan with raw materials. When this did not work, Japan invaded, took over French Indochina, and held it for the duration of the Second World War. This also gave the Japanese safe bases a thousand miles closer to their objectives in South-east Asia. The U.S. reacted by placing embargos on all exports of oil, steel and iron to Japan as a deterrent, but this actually made it more essential than ever for the Japanese to acquire these resources from elsewhere.

CHINA: THE WAR OF RESISTANCE
1938 – 1941

The Nationalist Party had never been in full control of all of China. There were many areas, especially in the north and west, which were still governed by independent militarists with their own armies. Their loyalties were always unpredictable, and they were likely to side with the Communists, if they had to make a choice, or even possibly the Japanese. For many years, the Nationalist government had been building railways and improving waterways to bring these remote areas a more modern way of life and to enable the government to develop more control over them. The Japanese recognized how strategically important these means of transport were to moving their troops around the country, and now made them their primary target. In January 1938, Japan had officially declared war on China and stepped up their offensive.

On April 8th, 1938, the Japanese attacked the city of Taierzhuang, situated on both the Grand Canal and a railway in Central China. Chiang's forces fought brilliantly, finally defeating the Japanese. This gave them a huge morale boost, and increased their confidence to try to push the Japanese back on other fronts. However, about five weeks later, the Japanese captured Suchow (Xuzhou), not far away in the Jiangsu Province, after a fierce battle. As this city was on the north-south railway, and the key to the defence of Hankow (Wuhan), it put the Nationalist headquarters in extreme danger. The enemy was now on the north shore of the Yellow River, close to

Chengchow (Zhengzhou) and the junction of the north-south and east-west railways.

Chiang faced the biggest crisis of his career. The Japanese defeat at Taierzhaung had caused them serious loss of face and they had celebrated their victory at Suchow with an orgy of murder, rape and arson, similar to Nanking. They were close to their goal, and Chiang knew that his forces could not stop their immediate advance on Hankow and his headquarters, however many bridges he sabotaged. He had no time left to evacuate the government and the hundreds of thousands of refugees who had settled in Hankow for protection. It was the biggest industrial city still under his control, and it was even possible that its fall might mean the loss of China as a nation. He only had one option left, but the results of this would be so horrific that it was almost beyond contemplation. However, Chiang Kai-shek and the Nationalist Government were desperate and decided that this option was the lesser of the two evils.

On June 8th, 1938, Chiang ordered a small group of engineers to breach the dikes on the Yellow River in complete secrecy. The result was devastating. A wall of water, a metre and a half high, fanned out southeast over fifty-four thousand square kilometres in central China. It killed about half a million people and left between three and five million refugees with nowhere to go. The farm animals died and the crops were lost, just as they were ripening, in one of the richest areas of farmland in China. Chiang announced to the world that the dams had been breached by Japanese aerial bombing. Japan denied this strongly, but both Chinese and foreigners were disinclined to give them the benefit of the doubt.

From the Nationalist's point of view, it accomplished two vital things. It stopped the enemy temporarily in its tracks, and gave the government another five months for an organised withdrawal to Chungking (Chongqing), further west on the Yangtze River in Szechuan Province. They dismantled government offices, factories, schools and even universities and loaded the equipment onto boats. They gathered the crops and farm animals from around Hankow, and all the stores in the granaries. It would be a long journey and they would need these supplies when they arrived in Chunking.

Some of the refugees went with them, but a large number decided to return to their homes in areas already captured by the Japanese, as probably being safer from attacks. The Japanese actually encouraged them to do this, as the millions of refugees wandering around the countryside were an administrative nightmare. An important and unplanned bonus from the rupture of the dam proved to be the publicity that it caused. The magnitude of the disaster shocked the world and made the Western countries aware of China's plight. On October 25th, 1938 the Japanese navy attacked and captured Hankow from the river, well supported by their air force, but by this time it was an almost empty city.

❀   ❀   ❀   ❀   ❀

The Nationalists were able to re-establish their headquarters in Chungking, but this was a foreign land to them and one that they had never really controlled. The dialects and diet of the Ba people were strange to Eastern Chinese, and the local population was unfriendly at first. The mountainous topography was very different from the fertile plains of east-central China and the Lower Yangtze valley. This was a land of mountains, cliffs, rivers, forests and limestone caves, and very little agriculture as they had known it. Chungking is upriver from the famous Three Gorges in the Wu Mountains, so is in beautiful and mysterious terrain. The climate is humid subtropical, with a high rainfall, a low number of sunny days each year, and about a hundred days of fog. It was not the capital of Szechuan, but had been the first treaty port to open up to foreign trade in the interior of China, so was not entirely unused to strangers.

The arrival of the Nationalists and their followers immediately overwhelmed the city's infrastructure and the available housing, necessitating the fast construction of a shanty town to accommodate them all. The only landing strip for aeroplanes was on a sand bar along the side of the Yangtze, and was only usable in dry weather. After heavy rain anywhere upstream, the sand bar was covered with water. Chiang realised that the Japanese could attack them by air, so shelters were an urgent priority. Luckily, the mountains around the city were full of limestone caves, and these proved ideal for this purpose.

They did not have to wait long to test the caves. The High Command in Japan had been outraged by the turn of events. Their armies had not captured the Nationalist government in Hanchow, as they had expected, and they had been left with miles of flooded, useless land and millions of refugees blocking all the roads out of the area. Japan had been relying on the excellent harvest to feed their troops in China, with enough left to export the extra to Japan. Now their troops were bogged down, the Chinese government had fled to safety, and Japan was being blamed unfairly by the world for breaking the dams.

In violent retribution, planes were sent to bomb Chungking in a reign of terror that continued until August 1943. The bombs specifically targeted the civilian population, and came whenever the weather was clear. The pattern of life in the city adapted to the weather. When it was foggy, people could go about their business, but on clear days they hid in the caves or other shelters and stayed there until dusk. Businesses and schools had to conform to this pattern and, in this way, the majority managed to survive, in spite of tens of thousands of deaths.

Not content with harassing the population of Chungking by air, the Japanese found ways to cut off the Chinese supply routes. They started by invading the southern provinces and severed the land routes to the sea, one by one. They then invaded Indochina in September 1940, and closed the railway that supplied that route. This left only the long and difficult road through Burma, and by flying supplies over the Himalayas, known as the Hump, from India. Both these were unpredictable and dangerous. Chungking felt very isolated and essential supplies like food and fuel were running short.

❀   ❀   ❀   ❀   ❀

After the initial attacks on Shanghai and Nanking in December 1937, Chiang Kai-shek had become aware of a ground swell of opinion arising throughout the country that China should try to negotiate a peace agreement with Japan. The realization that other cities might have to endure a slaughter like the Rape of Nanking was a challenge to the most patriotic of Chinese. Chiang was reluctant regarding this, but finally allowed Wang Ching-wei and Zhou Fohai to initiate informal talks with Japanese government representatives in Shanghai, to determine what terms the Japanese would be prepared to discuss. Wang had been second in command to Sun Yat-sen, so was an old friend and rival.

Meetings at many levels continued for more than two years and the Nationalist Party was severely split on the issue. Chiang found the Japanese terms too extreme for serious discussion and refused to consider them. However, Wang and Zhou felt that true patriots should try to make peace with Japan, as the only way to save China, so secretly formed a breakaway group. On March 30th, 1940, Wang Ching-wei, Zhou Fohai and their dissident party finally established a rival Nationalist government in Nanking under the patronage of the Japanese. They were officially recognized by Tokyo on November 30th of that year.

Recognising that the Nationalists were in a very fragile position, the United States came to their rescue with a financial loan, planes and other military equipment. This enabled them to hold on for a little longer, but Chiang knew that, without more help from other nations, they could not resist the Japanese indefinitely. He felt cut off from other parts of China and was continually nervous about allowing the Communists to acquire too much power, so commanded them to stay north of the Yellow River. For the two years from 1939 to 1941, Chiang found himself at war not only with the Japanese, but with the puppet regime in Nanking, some of the independent militarists and, at times, the Communists. However, he was determined to continue the War of Resistance, and would do this with very little outside help, until the end of 1941.

However, a consultant on his own staff, Claire L. Chennault, a retired U.S. army officer, came up with an intriguing idea. He formed the first American Volunteer Group (AVG). This had to be a clandestine operation, as the U.S. was not yet at war with Japan, but it had President Roosevelt's blessing. Pilots from various branches of the US forces were allowed to take leave of absence from their active units and volunteer for the AVG on terms similar to those of mercenaries. None-the-less, it was a US mission, seconded to China and organised by Chennault. Some aeroplanes that were about to be shipped to Britain were diverted for this, and the AVG team arrived in Burma complete with planes, parts, pilots and ground crews. They used a British base there and went into training during the summer and autumn of 1941. They then patrolled the Chinese supply lines along the Burma Road and helped to train Chinese pilots to defend Chungking. Immediately after Pearl Harbour, and the U.S. entry into the war, *The Flying Tigers*, as they were called, flew active missions in both Burma and China. They were famous for their courage and success in bringing down Japanese planes, and helped to make China feel that they were not fighting alone.

WHITE ROCK, BRITISH COLUMBIA
1941 - 1946

My parents finally succumbed to mounting pressure and my mother, Colin and I left China on the Japanese *SS Nitta Maru* for San Francisco, California on May 23rd, 1941.

We sat in the launch taking us out to the ship anchored in the middle of the river, and waved to my father standing alone on the dock. We hated leaving without him, but he had managed well by himself while we were in Hong Kong, and none of us really believed that the Japanese would actually challenge Britain, America and their allies to a full-scale war in the Pacific. We had been told that we would be back in a few months. However, the tears rolled down my cheeks as I remembered saying goodbye to Ah Wong, our baby amah, on the steps of our home in Tifeng Road. She had looked after Colin and me all our lives with love and patience. She had woken us in the morning, put us to bed at night and taken care of us through all the hours in between. She had gone on adventures with Ian and me into the markets of the Chinese city and to places that my parents had never been, and we were bonded to her by our secrets. Suddenly, I had a deep feeling that I would never see her again and knew that I would miss her with all my heart.

We clambered on board the *Nitta Maru*, left our things in our cabin and went up on deck to watch the ship sailing. As I leaned over the rail, I said goodbye to the city of my birth and stared at the slowly disappearing view of the Bund. I was only

10 years old, but I grew up in those few minutes and realised that I was leaving everything I loved and that was familiar behind. I knew that whatever people said, this was no temporary furlough, and that we were travelling into a foreign and unknown world. In fact, I never saw Shanghai again, although China would be part of my very being for the rest of my life.

My father must have been very relieved to know that his family was sailing to safety, and returned to his job. Like most of the other men in his position, he quickly closed down our home, moved into a small bachelor apartment and waited for what now seemed to be inevitable. We can only speculate on how those remaining foreigners felt, each of them with their own circumstances, but we know that Eric felt confident that he was performing an essential service and that he would probably be safe, even if the Japanese took over the International Settlement.

Unfortunately, my father, like so many others, underestimated the effects that the US sanctions were having on Japan, and how desperate they had become to find new sources of oil, steel and the other essentials that they needed so badly. Neither did they understand the full extent of the Japanese hatred for Western Imperialism in Asia and, in particular, the superiority and influence of the British and Americans there.

❀ ❀ ❀ ❀ ❀

We arrived safely in San Francisco on June 12th 1941. From there, we made our way north to Canada by bus. Originally, my mother had planned to go to Victoria, B.C., as she had some contacts there, but by the time we reached the border, we were exhausted from the journey. The first Canadian town the bus stopped at was White Rock and we decided to break the journey there. In those days, this was still a pretty little seaside town and seemed to offer everything that we needed to wait out the rest of the war, so we stayed.

We rented a house and Colin and I were enrolled in the local school for the new term in September. This was quite a cultural shock for both us and the children of White Rock! We had strange accents, talked about things they had never heard of, and were ahead in some classes and behind in others. We knew nothing about the local sports teams or current movies, pop songs and film stars. In fact, we were considered to be very weird and took a lot of teasing in the beginning. I was eventually accepted because I was a natural athlete and was soon playing on the school teams. However, poor Colin, who was only five years old and was starting primary school for the first time, found it much harder to adjust.

My father had given my mother a letter to mail to the head office of the Shanghai Power Company in the United States, when we finally found a place to settle. From then on they sent us a cheque every month so we were much better off than many others who had escaped from the pending war in Asia. For the first few months, mail came fairly regularly from father and he received the letters that we sent him. He was comfortable enough in his little apartment and Cookie and Amah were with him, although there was not much for them to do. He said war was imminent and that he was so glad to know that we were safe in Canada and had found such a friendly place to live.

The beach was a great source of fun, although I never got used to the cold water of the northern Pacific - so very different from the warm Chinese beaches that we were used to. However, a friend of the family taught us to fish off the pier, and even to cook the fish we caught right on the beach on a big flat stone over a little fire. Fish never tasted so good, before or after that. We also learned to catch shellfish in the rocky pools and dig for clams in the sand. These were delicious and it was fun to do. There were lots of seabirds to learn about, and the endless boat traffic to watch, so there were a lot of new and exciting things in our lives.

One day, some friends took us to buy fresh vegetables at a farm with a country market, and I was thrilled to find that it was owned and operated by a Chinese family. I chatted to the owner, Mr. Lee, and told him how we had just arrived from

China, and how homesick I was. He invited us to meet his family and before we left, asked me if I would like to work for him at weekends and after school. I immediately accepted and this became a very important part of my life from then on. The Lees were good people and we found lots of things to talk about while we were hoeing weeds or staking tomatoes. I not only made some very welcome pocket money, but I found a kindred spirit. In many ways, Mr. Lee became the father figure I needed so badly at that age.

※　※　※　※　※

Shortly before daybreak on Monday, December 8th, 1941 sporadic gunfire woke the residents of Shanghai. Many thought it was merely another fire cracker display set off to welcome a Chinese festival and went back to sleep. However, a cloud of black smoke rising from the Whangpoo River soon set off the alarm. The Japanese navy had approached the gunboat *USS Wake,* while her officers and many of the crew were still asleep on shore, and had quickly boarded her with little resistance. Trying to do the same with the British gunboat *HMS Petrel* had not been as easy. When the officer on duty resisted the Japanese boarding party, the gunboats nearby opened fire and sunk the *Petrel.* The crew jumped over-board and swam to the shore where they were arrested.

By the time most of the Shanghailanders had woken up, the Japanese had quietly taken over the Shanghai Municipal Council (SMC) offices, the police station, all essential utilities, the local radio station, and other buildings of strategic importance in the International Settlement and the French Concession. Sentries had been posted outside the consulates and all major foreign businesses. The British fleet had left Shanghai for Singapore the previous year, but the few remaining military personnel had been arrested. Downtown, the streets were full of armed Japanese troops, jostling with the usual early morning activities, and the traffic had jammed to a halt. Ships had blockaded the river downstream and the aerodromes had been secured, so any hope of escape was now useless.

The Japanese members of the SMC had access to lists of all the Shanghai residents and categorised them according to their priority. Some groups, like the Shanghai police, the secret service and specifically marked individuals, were arrested with their families immediately. Others, like my father, working in essential services, civic administration, and food supplies etc., were told to return to their jobs and were more or less free for about another year. Any thoughts of non-co-operation or sabotage were quickly dispelled by severe warnings from their new Japanese masters.

As those with wirelesses tuned in to the outside world, an event of even greater importance assaulted them. Japan had attacked the huge U.S. naval base at Pearl Harbour in Hawaii, inflicting enormous damages to the base and to the U.S. fleet. Being across the International Date Line, this happened just before 8.00 am on December 7th. As this was a Sunday, the ships were in harbour and most of the crews were asleep ashore. There were over 3,700 people killed or wounded. Within twenty-four hours, the United States of America declared war on Japan, Germany and the other Axis partners and joined forces with the Allies.

The magnitude of what had happened sank in slowly over the next few days and weeks as news kept pouring in. Within a few hours of the attack on Pearl Harbour, the Japanese had also bombed Singapore, Hong Kong and the Philippines and had landed troops in three locations along the Siamese (Thai) and Malayan boarder. They had captured the airport at Kota Bahru, divided east and west, and were slowly making their way south through the almost impenetrable Malayan jungle and rubber plantations. The following day, Japanese planes and torpedoes sank the *HMS Prince of Wales* and *HMS Repulse* off the South-east coast of Malaya. On December 11th, the island of Penang was bombed leaving over a thousand people killed and many more injured. A week later, Borneo

and Sarawak were under attack with some of the Indonesian
Islands soon to follow. On December 23rd, they took Wake Island in the Pacific. As the Americans in Pearl Harbour patched
up their wounded and buried their dead, millions of people in
South-east Asia and the Pacific were not only attacked, but
would have to struggle for their very existence under Japanese
occupation for the next three or four years.

❀   ❀   ❀   ❀   ❀

In White Rock, we were sitting at lunch with the radio playing
gentle music in the background on Sunday, 7th December.
Suddenly, this was interrupted by a news flash to say that the
Japanese Air Force had bombed Pearl Harbour. The following
day, we heard that the United States of America had entered
the war on the side of the Allies and had declared war on Japan
and her Axis partners. Over the next few days, the awful news
of the bombings of Honk Kong and Singapore were reported,
but no news of what was happening in Shanghai. We were
frantic and hoped the Lees could find out something for us
through the Chinese grapevine. We eventually heard through
this source that the Japanese had taken over all the treaty
ports in China, but nothing more specific. North American
broadcasters had more dramatic events to report, as the Japanese created havoc all over South-east Asia and the Pacific,
and the BBC was largely concerned with the war in Europe.

The months went by with no more than rumours; there
seemed to be no news at all about China on any radio channel
or in the newspapers. Then in September 1942, we suddenly
received a short letter from my father. This had been brought
to New York by one of the first repatriation ships and was
mailed to us from there. The relief was so intense, we all cried
for days. He was safe and well and was still working for the
Shanghai Power Company. His Japanese boss was a civilian
engineer and a decent man who was fluent in English. He said
he was fine and we were not to worry about him. He loved us
all very much and missed us badly. Things would be all right;

we just needed to be patient and enjoy our temporary lives in the safety of Canada. This was the last time we heard anything from or about him for a long time.

For almost five years, I would be the man of the house in this new country. My mother made some good friends among the local ladies and they became very supportive. She suddenly had to learn to cook, clean the house and look after her children on her own. This must have been hard on her at first but she took it in her stride, with a lot of help from her new friends. The thing that bothered her most was managing her money, for she had no idea what the future would bring, and no experience at this. She insisted on being very frugal and saving as much of our monthly income as she could, which meant that there was little money for luxuries, but we had a simple and comfortable life style, and slowly learned to be Canadians.

PHOTOGRAPHS

Catherine (Kate) McDonald Duncan. 1862-1919.
Kate married Albert Colterjahn in 1889 and brought the first Scottish blood into the Colterjahn family. They had three sons: William, Samuel John Duncan, and Albert Eric, and one daughter, Jean.

Emily (Amy) Dunthie. 1905-1993

Albert Eric Colterjohn. 1889-1973

Eric & Amy

Eric & Amy's Wedding Party

Amy at her wedding in Shanghai, 1929

Eric, Amy & Duncan

Eric, Amy, Duncan & Colin. Scotland, 1939

Maureen's Birthday, 1937. With Sam, Mary, and Ian

Sam and Family

Elizabeth (Libby) Shaen Orr

Dr. Eric Duncan Colterjohn (1930-2005)

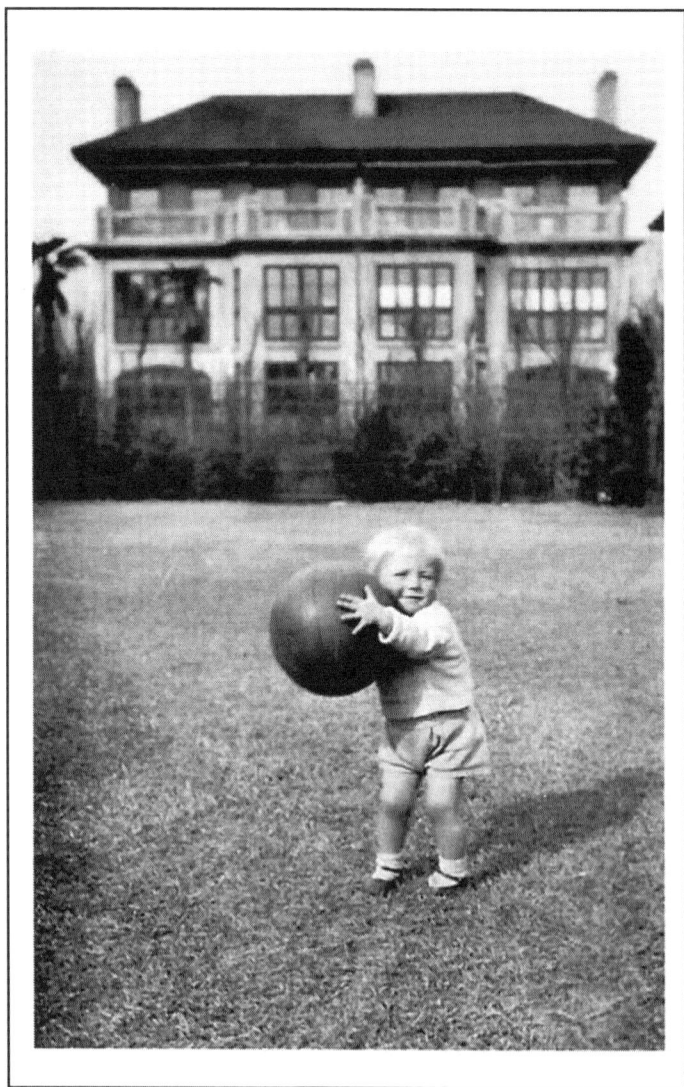

Duncan at Tifeng Road House. 1932

WAR IN ASIA

1941 – 1943

With the Japanese occupation of Shanghai, things deteriorated quickly for the 8,000 remaining residents from Allied countries. They were told to register at the new Enemy Aliens Office, where they were given armbands with their individual registration number and a large letter indicating their nationality, as in "B" for British. This meant standing in long lines in all weather, sometimes for days on end, and they had to wear these whenever they went out. All foreigners were forbidden to go to hotels, restaurants, cinemas, clubs and other forms of entertainment. Their cars and, in many cases, their homes were confiscated and they were forced to share accommodation. All foreign businesses were taken over by the Japanese and the bank accounts drained. Personal bank accounts were frozen and foreigners were only allowed to withdraw a very small amount each month during a two-hour period daily. All these measures were intended to humiliate the Westerners and to bring their standard of living down to that of poor Chinese.

Allied diplomats were immediately rounded up and put under house arrest at the Cathay Mansions in the French Concession. Japanese naval officers took over the Shanghai Club, and the American Club became their naval headquarters. Suddenly, these proud Westerners had fallen from the top of the social ladder to close to the bottom. They could no longer afford servants or to heat their cramped quarters, and found themselves learning to clean, cook and wash, many for the first time in their lives. They had to travel by public transport, or bicycle if they were lucky, and to fight for rice, fish and vegetables in the Chinese markets. A serious shortage of basic foods developed within the first few months, due to the famine all over China, while the Japanese, Germans and Italians grew fat from the black market. Most frightening of all was the establishment of the new Kempei Tei detention centre in the Bridge House in Hongkew. People were arrested from all walks of life for apparently no reason, and very few survived the torture and appalling conditions there. However, hard as all this was, they were still living in comparative freedom and comfort compared to what was to come.

✹   ✹   ✹   ✹   ✹

News from the rest of South-east Asia and the Pacific continued to get worse. The garrison and civilians on Hong Kong fought bravely with virtually no sea or air backup, but finally surrendered on Christmas Day 1941. In January 1942, the Japanese invaded Burma, New Guinea and the Solomon Islands and in February, sunk the US aircraft carrier *Langley*. Many other Allied ships, including the huge U.S. warship *Houston*, were bombed and torpedoed. Bali and Timor fell in February and Java and Sumatra surrendered in March. The Philippines struggled on until May 8th, but eventually the U.S. lost their big air force base there. In March and April, there was a wave of air raids against Ceylon, which also sank the British aircraft carrier *HMS Hermes* and other Allied ships. On February 19th, a large force Japanese aircraft bombed Darwin, and continued with intermittent attacks on the north and east coastal cities of Australia until November 1943. The Australians managed to hold on, in spite of having sent great numbers of troops all over the Pacific and South-east Asia to fight with other Allied forces.

Singapore, the citadel and bastion of British naval strength in South-east Asia, turned into one of the worst fiascos in British military history. Everything that could go wrong did. The people on the island refused to believe that the Japanese would dare to attack Singapore. However, the Japanese marched 400 miles from their landings on the Siamese-Malayan border, capturing Kuala Lumpur and other strategic points en route, and attacked Singapore from mainland Malaya, across the Straits of Jahore. They brought tanks and artillery with them and were fully supported by air. On February 15th, 1942, Singapore capitulated.

⊛   ⊛   ⊛   ⊛   ⊛

In early summer of 1942, excitement spread throughout Shanghai with the news that negotiations were taking place for the exchange of prisoners. With 8,000 Allied civilians still in Shanghai, the competition was fierce, especially as people from the interior of China were also on the list. In June, the Italian ship *Conte Verde*, which had been stranded in Shanghai since the war in Asia started, sailed with about 600 Americans and Canadians on board. She was accompanied by the *Asama Maru*, carrying Allied internees from Japan and South-east Asia, to rendezvous with the *MS Gripsholm* in Lourenco Marques, Mocambique, where they exchanged passengers. They sailed for New York from there on July 28th with 1,510 people on board, including over 100 children.

The MS Gripsholm was built in England for the Swedish American Line. When she was launched in 1925, she was the first ocean liner to be equipped with diesel engines, which were faster and cheaper to run than the conventional steam. She was chartered to the US State Department during the Second World War, from 1942 to 1946, as an exchange and repatriation ship, under the protection of the Red Cross, and had "diplomat" painted in huge letters on both sides. When she sailed at night, she was lit up brightly to distinguish her as a mercy ship. The Japanese ships, with which she exchanged prisoners, had to do the same.

In August, the *Kamakura Maru* sailed with about 200 British diplomats and civilians. This was to be the only repatriation to Britain, as the west coast of North America was much more accessible across the Pacific Ocean. Also, Britain, unlike the US, did not take many Japanese prisoners. Her principal role in the Asian war was to defend her Empire and to assist her allies, rather than to attack the Japanese.

❀   ❀   ❀   ❀   ❀

My father, Eric was not among those repatriated but had been luckier than many so far. The Japanese engineer who had been sent to the Shanghai Power Company to work with him and learn his job, was a civilian and a cultured man who had lived in Edinburgh, Scotland for three years. In fact, by strange co-incidence, they had both attended the Herriot Watt Engineering College there, so they had this in common. Although circumstances made it impossible for them to become friends, they were able to work together.

Shortly before Eric was sent to a Civilian Assembly Centre, the Japanese engineer told him a story: apparently, the SS *Nitta Maru*, with my mother, Colin and me on board, had been selected to provide one of the *incidents* that would give justification for the much greater act of aggression against the U.S. fleet in Pearl Harbour. As the *Nitta Maru* was a Japanese ship carrying American and British evacuees, she was to have been sunk by the Japanese after she entered U.S. territorial waters, and the United States would have been blamed for doing this. As luck would have it, the submarine developed engine trouble and our ship docked safely in San Francisco. We cannot substantiate this story, but my father had no doubts regarding its authenticity, and it was typical of the Japanese *modus operandi*.

❀   ❀   ❀   ❀   ❀

As owning a short wave radio was a seriously punishable offense, those foreigners still living in Shanghai heard very little of what was going on in the rest of the world. In fact, nations were hopping in and out of bed with each other with the speed of whores. A non-aggression pact signed one month was violated the next and it was hard enough for those in Europe to follow what was happening in the war. In April 1941, the Japanese signed a non-aggression pact with Soviet Russia, encouraged by the fact that their Tripartite partner, Germany, had done the same in 1939. However, in June 1941, Germany launched Operation Barbarossa against the Soviets breaking their treaty. They invaded with three million troops along 1,000 mile frontier. Russia made overtures to China to help, but the USA and Britain feared that an alliance of that size could destabilize world politics further, especially after the war ended, so advised against this.

Throughout 1942, the U.S.A. and Britain were concerned with keeping China on the side of the Allies and started negotiations to relinquish their extraterritorial rights in China, as a means of strengthening their friendship. Hong Kong had been given to Britain "in perpetuity", so was not part of this. Agreements between Britain and China, and the U.S.A. and China, were finally signed on January 11th, 1943 to come into full effect when the war ended. This not only returned the treaty ports to China, it contained clauses repealing the Chinese Exclusion Act in the U.S.A. and the Boxer Protocol of 1901. It provided for special trade agreements for the U.S.A. and Britain, but essentially, Shanghai was part of China again from that date. With all the confusion of the war surrounding them, most Shanghailanders did not hear about this until they were liberated in 1945.

CHINA: AN ALLIED PARTNER
1941 – 1944

The Japanese attacks all over Asia were the beginning of grandiose plans for a Greater East Asia Co-Prosperity Sphere to be governed by Japan. They had been planning this since the end of the Great War. In 1922, at the height of the British Empire, Britain had influence over about one-fifth of the world's population and almost a quarter of the total land mass, coloured pink on the maps. Although the Japanese resented the British and everything that they stood for, Japan was also stimulated by what another small country had achieved, and this nurtured the seeds of imperialism in the Japanese mind. Originally, Japan had visualized conquering China first, to meet her immediate needs, and then slowly expanding over Asia. However, China had proved to be much more resilient than she had expected and Japan needed to move on to other goals. With a rapidly expanding population and the U.S. sanctions on oil, steel and iron hurting the economy, Japan needed the rubber and tin from Malaya and oil from Borneo. In fact, Japan could not even grow enough food to feed its own people.

As the war dragged on in Europe, Japan realised that the time was right to implement further action. Britain and Europe were totally extended in their own war effort, and they assumed that the United States would eventually become involved in this too. Troops from all over the British Empire had been sent to Europe, even from Australia, India and South-east

Asia, reducing opposition to invasion in these areas. Japan was aware that there was unrest in many of the Asian countries governed by Britain, and that they were clamouring for independence. She hoped that they would welcome Japanese assistance to throw off the yoke of British Imperialism and to join an all-Asian alliance. It shocked them to discover that, in spite of wanting their independence, these countries remained loyal to the British Empire. Japan was trying to capture the hearts and minds of other Asian countries by invasion over a few months, failing to understand that it had taken the British centuries to build their Empire, largely through diplomacy and trade.

It is a misconception to suggest that the war in Europe *spread* to Asia, as they were two separate theatres of conflict. Although Japan was an Axis partner, the Japanese never assisted their European associates or fought alongside them. Japan took advantage of the fact that European countries, like Britain, Russia and France, were too preoccupied with the war in Europe to be able to defend their possessions in Asia properly, making it a perfect time for Japan to invade her Asian neighbours. However, the causes and motivations for the war with Japan were completely different from those that started the war in Europe.

The culture and the priorities of the Japanese at this time were so different from the West, that it is important to understand a little about these. Since the end of the Great War, Japan had only one goal; to become the strongest military power in Asia, if not the whole world. To the Japanese mind, there were only two kinds of people; the strong and the weak, and the strong had the right to take all. However, to achieve this she needed to expand into neighbouring territories to supply her basic needs for natural resources. Everything about the Japanese way of life was geared towards this military objective. Martial arts were part of the school curriculum from an early age and secondary school boys were taught to use guns. By late 1943, the population was starving and schools were being turned into munitions factories with the students working there. Boys aged 14, and sometimes younger, were conscripted into the armed forces.

❀   ❀   ❀   ❀   ❀

After December 1941, the Japanese quickly took over the other treaty ports in China. The invading force was now in control of a wide swath of eastern China from Manchuria and Peking to Canton and Hong Kong. As the aggressive ambitions of the Japanese towards all of Asia increased, the United States decided that a strong Chinese ally was of utmost importance. Chiang Kai-shek and the Nationalist Government were still in unoccupied territory, so the U.S. government was able to send financial aid, arms and equipment to assist them in the War of Resistance against the Japanese. They also made China a member of the Allied Nations *Big Four*. This gave Chiang a chance to show his strength as a statesman, and he went to India to visit the national leaders there in February 1942. Nehru had been to China in 1939, so Chiang had already developed a good relationship with him. Chiang's message to India was clear. They must support the Allied forces in their war effort to defeat the Japanese, and then concentrate on achieving their independence.

General George C. Marshall, Chief of Staff of the American army, favoured a "Europe first" strategy, so the United States did not send troops to China. Instead, they appointed an American Chief of Staff to command the Chinese forces under the ultimate authority of Chiang Kai-shek, hoping to provide the maximum efficiency available to defend China. General Joseph Warren Stilwell arrived in Chungking in March 1942 to take up this post. He was horrified at the condition of the Chinese troops that he was to command. They were underfed, under equipped, badly trained and poorly educated. They had been fighting the Japanese since 1937, largely without support from outside China, and were exhausted. He complained that the Generals had too much autonomy, the chain of command was too loose and the officers were corrupt and undisciplined. These were all true, but it was the reality of China at that time.

Instead of working with Chiang to build up the condition of the troops to better defend China, Stilwell saw them merely as a disposable asset. He ordered them to Burma to support the British in the fight against the Japanese there, as this was an important buffer between China and British India. This put Chiang in a difficult position. He was grateful for U.S. aid and their support, but had not anticipated having to send his troops out of China. However, he was still receiving great quantities of supplies via the Burma Road, which he realised needed to be kept open, so co-operated with Stilwell's plans.

Months of disaster followed with constant disagreements between the two leaders. Stilwell accused Chiang of being too defensive, and only wanting to maintain his supply lines and to protect his troops. Chiang accused Stilwell of lack of experience in the field, being too aggressive and taking unwarranted risks without proper strategy. These were probably all true, but caused a triangle of mutual distrust with the British, at a time when they should have been pulling together to fight the Japanese. Eventually, this ended in defeat on all fronts for the Allies. The Chinese supply lines were cut off and their regiments took huge losses. Stilwell managed to make his way north through dense jungle to India with a miscellaneous group of people of several nationalities and a few remnants of the Chinese army. He was still in control of the U.S. *lend-lease* for China, which he now used on other projects as he saw fit.

The remainder of the Chinese troops limped back to Chungking and Chiang finally turned his attention to matters at home. Chunking was now seriously isolated with all the supply routes cut off, except by flying fuel and provisions in from India over *the Hump*. The first two years of the war with Japan had seen abundant crops all over the country, but 1941 and 1942 provided drought and famine, partly as a result of the breaching of the Yellow River dams. Chiang ordered land taxes to be paid in grain, so that he could feed his army, but this caused even greater hardship for the peasants and a lasting resentment of the Nationalists, especially in the rich farm areas of Hunan. In contrast, the Communists had started a policy of self-efficiency in the areas they held so, although everyone was starving, the people were slightly better off there and would support the Communists later. In all, about four million people had died of starvation by the end of 1942.

⊛   ⊛   ⊛   ⊛   ⊛

War-torn China had three distinct areas of authority. Chiang Kai-shek commanded the Nationalist government from Chunking, which was still unoccupied by the Japanese, with the assistance of the Americans. Mao Tse-tung commanded the Communists from their base in Yan'an in north-west China, with some of his troops behind enemy lines in remote areas fighting with guerrilla tactics. Wang Ching-wei had set up a puppet government in Nanking, in collaboration with the Japanese, and was administering Japanese-held areas. All three had their own armies and intelligence sectors, which were capable of instilling terror and using violent methods to extract information. Added to these were several areas in the north and west that had never been really under Nationalist authority and were governed by independent militarists with their own armies. These were devious and unpredictable and could just as easily support the Japanese as either the Nationalists or the Communists, so Chiang could not rely on them.

Although the Nationalists and the Communists were supposed to be fighting the Japanese together under the banner of the United Front, in fact they were conducting their separate wars, with very different methods, both with an eye to capturing as much of China as possible when the war with Japan ended. Chiang had cut off the government subsidy to the Communists back in 1940, as he still considered them his greatest threat in the long term. From then on, Mao started to develop his own plans for the future and, in February 1942, announced his new Rectification Movement.

In Chunking, things were even more complicated and it had become a hotbed of intrigue. General Stilwell had been joined by several other U.S. generals and American advisors, each with their own field of expertise and intelligence departments, and each reporting to separate people in Washington. On the whole, they guarded their areas of authority jealously and rarely shared their intelligence.

The relationship between Chiang and Stilwell had continued to worsen since the debacle in Burma, and Stilwell frequently disagreed with the other American advisors too, which created its own problems. Stilwell had the ears and eyes of President Roosevelt, and sent endless communiqués criticising Chiang, which created a biased view in Washington of what was happening in China. Chiang was often supported by General Chennault and Ambassador Patrick Hurley, but it was Stilwell he had to work with most closely. Most of the country was starving, the troops were underfed and demoralised and Chungking was being bombed consistently by the Japanese air force. Chiang must have been under high stress trying to manage all this and still stay on friendly terms with the Americans.

❀   ❀   ❀   ❀   ❀

In the spring of 1944, Japan invaded Burma in Operation Ugo. Stilwell once again ordered Chinese troops to participate. Chiang felt that this was a diversion for a final assault on China, and tried to insist that his troops remain in China to defend it, but was ordered by President Roosevelt to co-operate with Stilwell. The Allies finally defeated the Japanese in the Burmese campaign in June 1944, reopening those supply routes, but it was too little too late for China. Four out of every five Chinese soldiers were killed or severely injured.

Concurrently, Japan made an all-out attack on south-central China in Operation Ichigo. Chiang had been right in his forecast of this and was caught with vast numbers of his best troops in Burma. On top of this, peasants in Hunan province attacked Chinese soldiers and removed their weapons. They were reacting to years of abuse from the Nationalist armies, the breaking of the dikes in 1938, and the grain taxes imposed on them during the subsequent famine. The Japanese did not take Chungking and the western provinces, but they did immeasurable damage to the east, central and south parts of the country.

In Washington, Stilwell's endless complaints about Chiang started a movement to consider alternative Chinese leaders. In July 1944, a group of Americans were sent to Yan'an to talk to Mao Tse-tung. They found him co-operative and charming and admired the order and discipline of his troops, unaware of the Rectification Movement, which was slowly defining the future of the Communist party. In fact, Mao had no more intention of working closely with the Americans than they did of replacing Chiang, but everyone was hedging their bets with an eye to post-war China.

General Stilwell was recalled to Washington in October 1944. It appears he never learned to understand China or the Oriental mind, especially Chiang Kai-shek's. However, the enormous number of negative reports that he sent back to Washington, not only influenced the then current policy, but would also bias historical researchers for years to come. Chiang Kai-shek was no saint, and the corruption in the Nationalist Party would compromise him indefinitely but, after about 60 years, his positive contributions to the war in Asia have begun to be appreciated by the world at large. He was certainly the only man in China who could have held the country together at that time. China has also come to recognise this. Although the Communists indubitably won the peace, the victory against the Japanese was a multifaceted effort and it is indisputable that Chiang led the War of Resistance against Japan for eight years, in spite of enormous odds.

INTERNMENT
1943 – 1946

By January 1943, things started to get worse for those foreigners remaining in Shanghai. The Jews were gradually assembled and confined in a small area of Hongkew, although they were not actually imprisoned and could get passes to work in other areas. Nazi Germany put very heavy pressure on Japan to follow Germany's policy of *The Final Solution*, and it is to Japan's credit that they refused to cooperate with this. Many of the White Russian refugees were also allowed to remain relatively free, as long as they provided services for the Japanese. Most of them lived in the French Concession, which was now administered by the Vichy Government, and they were needed to run the restaurants and other places of entertainment for the benefit of the occupying forces. As unpleasant as this was, it was preferable to the alternative. From mid-January, the remaining residents from Allied Nations, who had not already been incarcerated, were rounded up and confined in Civilian Assembly Centres (CAC) - a nice name for atrocious prison camps.

The Japanese commandeered a number of large properties in and around Shanghai that they designated as CACs. Although they varied a lot in size, location and previous use, they had many things in common. They were mostly abandoned buildings with minimal facilities, filthy and in very poor condition, except for the religious institutions. Prisoners were moved into these with no prior attempts to prepare them for habitation, and the Japanese provided no tools or construction materials for the inmates to improve and clean the buildings themselves. They had to rely entirely on their own skills and initiative. Prisoners were usually allowed to take as much as they could carry with them into the camps, and it must have been interesting to note other peoples' priorities.

It appears that the authorities were organised in how they allocated internees to the various camps. The Franciscan House, The Sacred Heart, the Senmouyeu Nuns' Residence and Zikawei were all Catholic institutions and only priests, brothers and nuns were interned in these. Most of the former employees of the Shanghai Municipal Council went to either the Yu Yuen Road or to the Ash Camp, which was smaller than the others but had cubicles for family groups. A large number of Americans went to the Great China University in Chapei, where the buildings had been badly damaged in the bombing of 1937. The large Lunghwa Camp was in the former Chinese Kiansu Middle School, close to the Lunghwa Aerodrome, and had 59 dormitories for single men and 127 rooms for families with various backgrounds. Probably the most infamous was the Haiphong Road camp in the former barracks of a U.S. marine regiment. Most of the internees were prominent citizens and people of influence in fields of finance, politics and information who could cause problems for the Japanese. This was closely allied with the Bridge House, and prisoners were often taken there to be interrogated by the Kempei Tei.

⊛   ⊛   ⊛   ⊛   ⊛

At the end of January 1943, my father and the other foreign employees at the Shanghai Power Company were ferried across the Whangpoo River to the old British American Tobacco Company (BAT) factory near Pootung Point. When BAT built their new plant, the old buildings, which had been constructed in 1901, were used for warehousing until 1937, when they were closed down and condemned after the Japanese bombing as being unsafe. Although they had not received a direct hit, the adjacent Chinese village had been destroyed and the old factory had received collateral damage. It consisted of a main three-story brick building with a large red water tower on top. It also had 2 two-storey wings and a machine house, connected by covered walkways. All the buildings were in terrible condition, filthy, and full of bugs, rats and debris. There was an area of vacant land, about the size of three football fields, but this was heavily indented with bomb craters and covered with ruined buildings and rubble. There was also a pond of stagnant water full of mosquito larvae. The compound was surrounded by a high concrete wall topped with barbed wire.

The Pootung Camp originally housed about 1,100 single men: bachelors, men married to Asian or non-Allied nationals, and those who had evacuated their wives and families before the outbreak of war. They were predominately British and mostly came from the utility companies and essential services; others were private company executives, some ships' crews and even about 20 university professors. There were a large number of engineers and, on the whole, they were an intelligent, resourceful group of men determined to survive. Eric, at the age of 43, and with a job that was largely in administration by this time, was not as young or as fit as some, but he was an experienced engineer and a born entrepreneur. After the Japanese took over Shanghai, foreigners could no longer play tennis or golf but Eric had ridden his bicycle to work each day, which had helped him to stay in shape.

As the buildings were too dirty and full of debris to be habitable, the prisoners had no option but to start to clean them immediately. The only tools they had were those that they brought with them, as not even brooms were supplied. The plumbing in the buildings had always been very basic and was now unusable, so digging latrines outside became a priority. It was January and very cold; many of the windows were broken and there was no electricity. The main building housed 16 dormitories, and personal space was only 4' by 10', marked with chalk on the floor, but at least they had that. They worked for weeks cleaning, repairing and constructing water boilers and plumbing pipes, and providing cooking facilities. Slowly they could see the results of their efforts.

The machine building became the chapel, library, theatre and games room. The main dining room also housed the Poo-tung University, offering more than 150 courses covering a wide spectrum of interests. These were voluntarily organised by the resident professors, who even awarded credits through St. John's University in Shanghai for those who passed the examinations. There were no text books, paper or other learning tools, but the Japanese gave them some chalk and small pieces of charcoal, with which they could write on the walls. An interesting newspaper article has survived giving details of this unique school.

The internees levelled and cleaned up the surrounding vacant land to make garden plots and playing fields, which they called the *Happy Garden*. It was a place to get away from the crowded space inside and get some exercise. My father spent a lot of time in his garden trying to grow anything that he could to improve their diet. He found some wild dandelions, nettles and other weeds amongst the debris while they were clearing the ground, which he carefully saved and planted later. One of the university professors was a botanist and was very helpful with showing people what they could eat and what was poisonous. Whenever the cooks received a supply of potatoes, Eric persuaded them to let him cut out a few of the eyes and planted them too. The soil was very poor, mixed with building rubble including lime, and they had so very few things to grow. How he longed for some packets of certified vegetable seeds and a big pile of rich horse manure! After a Red Cross parcel arrived, he saved some seeds from a tin of tomatoes and was immensely proud when they actually grew.

Among the items that Eric brought into the camp were two packs of playing cards, a mouth organ, a Swiss army knife, a bundle of pencils, a pair of scissors, and small pick which had previously been used for gardening. With the scissors, he set himself up as a camp barber, which he found useful as trading currency. With the mouth organ, he joined the orchestra and became really skilled with it, even in classical pieces. With the pick, he created his garden and it had so many other uses that he had to watch it was not stolen. However, it was the playing cards that made his life most bearable. He joined a group that played serious bridge for several hours a day, and felt that this is what saved his sanity in those terrible years of filth and starvation. He also enrolled in several courses at the Pootung University, which he enjoyed very much as a diversion.

�   ✦   ✦   ✦   ✦

In early September 1943, another group was repatriated to the United States and Canada. They left Shanghai on the *Teia Maru*, which exchanged 1,500 Allied prisoners from Asia for 1,330 Japanese prisoners on board the *MS Gripsholm* in the port of Mormugao, in Portuguese India. The *Gripsholm* arrived safely in New Jersey on December 1st, 1943 carrying, not only her precious cargo of people, but many bags of mail from those left behind in the camps. For most of the families in North America, this was the first news they had received from their friends and relatives interned in China. A large amount of medical supplies and packaged food was transferred from the *Gripsholm* to the *Teia Maru* to be taken back to Shanghai for the internees of the CACs, but it is doubtful whether any of this ever reached the intended destinations. After the war, thousands of Red Cross parcels were found in warehouses undelivered. One hundred and fifty-four prisoners from Pootung were sent home with this group, but not my father.

However, just before Christmas 1943, in White Rock, my mother received a kind note from a stranger who told us he had just been repatriated to the U.S. and that he had been in Pootung CAC with my father. He said conditions were not good but that Dad was well and in good spirits. We were overjoyed with this news, bad as it was. At least we knew where he was and that he was alive. We heard nothing more until the end of the war.

About the same time, many of the younger and stronger men were transferred from Pootung to other camps as labour gangs. The vacancies were immediately filled, mostly from the CACs A and B at Yangchow, which were then closed. A number of women were among these new arrivals, changing the demographics of the camp considerably. Those who had been at Pootung from the beginning found these changes upsetting. For over seven months they had worked together to create a place in which they could survive, and had achieved so much that they had bonded as a group. They had learned to respect each other's strengths and weaknesses and had drawn a sense of security from the familiar, even in such terrible circumstances. This was now shattered. They found it hard to accept the new people, who did not understand their rules and way of doing things, and had not helped to create their environment.

Some of the men found the arrival of women particularly disconcerting in their all male domain. Others welcomed them and, no doubt, some will have taken advantage of their presence. The new situation created jealousies, rivalries and even the odd fight over the smallest detail. It was certainly not the new people's fault. They felt lost and insecure in their new surroundings and only wanted to quietly survive the rest of the war years. The guards were quick to pick up on these new tensions and responded by stepping up discipline. While the prisoners had exerted all their energy into cleaning and developing their surroundings into something habitable, the guards had shown some leniency, and occasionally even some help, but no longer. Many activities they had previously condoned became punishable offenses. Internees were frequently treated severely, for no other reason than to show that the guards were in charge.

The biggest problems were the lack of nutritious food, medical supplies, and the endless dirt. The old walls continually shed plaster dust and debris and the residents had nothing with which to kill the bugs and rats in the crowded conditions.

A small cut inflicted while gardening could quickly become septic and life-threatening, with no disinfectant to treat it. As the months went by, the daily rations were reduced and the thin gruel that they lived on contained less and less food value. Even the guards were managing on very small rations. People got ill easily and it became harder to do any form of physical work, especially in the heat and humidity of the summer. Every day, there were a few more deaths from starvation, the lack of medicines, or abuse from the guards. The morale of the guards deteriorated as it became obvious to them that the war was not going in their favour, and they took out their frustrations on the prisoners.

In July 1944, they saw the first U.S. planes flying reconnaissance flights over the city. In November, the U.S. started to bomb strategic locations in Shanghai like the docks. By July 1945, these were daily events. Conditions in all the camps were appalling but the realization that the Americans were close improved morale and gave most of them the strength to hold on a little longer.

After the war, my father talked about many aspects regarding those years in Pootung Civilian Assembly Centre, but was reluctant to discuss the cruelty and disrespect with which the guards treated the internees. He said that was something he had to put behind him. However, one day in about 1952, he went with his lawn bowling club to an away match and refused to play until they cut each of the Japanese flags out of the bunting adorning the clubhouse. To me, this said more than a thousand words.

GOD BLESS THE AMERICANS
1945 – 1946

On August 6th, 1945, my 15th birthday, the U.S. Air Force dropped an atomic bomb on Hiroshima, Japan. A second bomb was dropped on Nagasaki on August 9th. The total number of deaths caused by these two bombs was about 240,000 - less than the number of Chinese soldiers and civilians raped and murdered by the Japanese in six weeks during the Rape of Nanking, in December 1937. Devastating as these atomic bombs were, they almost certainly inflicted fewer deaths and casualties on both sides than would have been caused by a conventional invasion of Japan. The Japanese Emperor Hirohito surrendered on August 15th, and broadcast on the radio worldwide to his loyal citizens and armed forces serving abroad. The war with Japan had ended.

❋　❋　❋　❋　❋

As it gradually became apparent that the Allies were going to win, both in Europe and in Asia, the dance of the politicians heated up. Each Allied country got ready for a land grab and jostled for the most advantageous position to fight the coming peace. Britain and the United States had already acknowledged that their next enemy would be Stalin and Communism in the USSR; thus the Cold War had started even before the Second World War ended. Chiang Kai-shek had hoped to take possession of Hong Kong after the Japanese surrendered, and return it to China. The British anticipated this and flew their troops in immediately, re-establishing their ownership of the island. They had lost their Chinese treaty ports and could not afford to lose their one remaining foothold in China.

Chiang wasted no time in trying to establish his control over the cities that had been under Japanese occupation, especially Shanghai, and enlisted the help of the U.S. Air Force to fly Nationalist personnel into Shanghai, Nanking and Peking. He wanted to take command and to accept the surrender from the Japanese before the Communist forces could do this. He was so afraid of the Red Army reaching Shanghai before his troops did, that he asked the Japanese to remain to administer and police the city until the American forces arrived.

This gave the Japanese plenty of time to destroy all recriminating documents and to load their ships with the loot they had confiscated from Shanghai. This included vast quantities of horded rice and other supplies, which they took home with them to Japan. In spite of Chiang's precautions, the Communists did manage to reach Manchuria and many of the northern Chinese cities ahead of the Nationalists, and accepted the Japanese surrender in these places. This provided them with rich prizes of weapons, artillery and the other tools of war. From then on, they called themselves the Peoples' Liberation Army (PLA).

❁   ❁   ❁   ❁   ❁

For the hundreds of thousands of prisoners from the Allied countries, their joy and relief was quickly followed by confusion and, in many cases, worse conditions than before. It has been estimated that well over 130,000 civilians, divided into approximately 50,000 men, 42,000 women and 40,000 children were still alive in more than 350 camps scattered all over South-east Asia, China, and Japan, and that at least 14,000 had died in the camps. As well, about 190,000 British and Commonwealth troops were still being held as prisoners-of-war. These numbers can never be completely verified, and are considered conservative by many, as there were a large num-

ber of small camps hidden up country in jungle areas, especially in Malaya and Burma, of which the liberating forces were
unaware. The job of rescuing these people was one of the biggest operations of the war in Asia and, in some cases, would
take many months.

The first priority was to feed all these prisoners until they
could be rescued, as the Japanese no longer took responsibility
for this after they surrendered. One of the conditions of the
surrender package was that the Japanese had to mark all the
POW camps and CACs so that they could be clearly recognised
from the air. From August 27th to September 20th, the U.S. Air
Force ran 900 sorties dropping 4,470 tons of emergency supplies to 158 camps in China, Korea and Japan alone.

B-29 planes, marked clearly with "PW SUPPLIES" flew over
the camps in three increments and dropped food, clothing and
medical supplies in metal canisters attached to parachutes.
Each plane was loaded with 10,000 pounds, separated into 40
individual drop units, and flew at about 1,000 feet with a speed
of 165 mph. For some areas, smaller planes had to be used
with less capacity. Although these conditions allowed them to
be fairly accurate with their drops, the internees had fierce
competition with local Chinese peasants, marauding bandits
and black market profiteers if they landed outside the camps.
Everyone, free or interned, was starving.

Pootung was definitely one of the luckiest camps, largely
because its location close to the shore of the Whangpoo River
across from the Bund made it very visible. The huge white
cross showed up well on the red tower, and the open space of
the playing field and the Happy Garden made a perfect drop
zone. The upper floor windows gave the internees a grand-
stand view of the river traffic over the next few weeks, and they
were able to cheer the U.S. fleet as it arrived to rescue them.
Immediately after the surrender, the prison guards disappeared from all the camps leaving the residents to fend for
themselves. Some tried to leave, but soon found that the outside world was a very dangerous place, and that staying in the

camps to wait for the Americans was a much safer decision. There is little doubt that, without those emergency drops, many more of them would have died of starvation before they could have been rescued.

Eventually, the U.S. ships sailed up the Whangpoo and systematically liberated camp by camp and took the internees to holding areas in Shanghai, where they could be given food and medical care. Pootung was one of the earliest camps to be evacuated, as the records show that my father was discharged in August 1945, although it is almost certain to have been mid-September before he left the camp.

❋   ❋   ❋   ❋   ❋

Over the next few months, many thousands of Americans arrived in Shanghai, where they were billeted awaiting repatriation. They had had a tough war in the Pacific and this was their first leave in a long time. They thronged the city with wallets stuffed with spending money looking for rest, rehabilitation and fun. This not only kick-started the local economy, especially the entertainment business, but it also brought smiles back to the faces of the community. Their enthusiasm, joy and youth lit the pilot light and things sparked back to life in Shanghai. With the troops came enormous amounts of food, medicine, jeeps and a plethora of American goods from the United Nations Relief and Rehabilitation Administration (UNRRA).

As the rescued internees slowly regained their health, they were able to find out what had been happening to other people for all those years that they had been locked up without news. It was a huge relief to hear that the war in Europe had ended, with Germany and their Axis partners surrendering unconditionally on May 8th of that year. However, one can imagine their shock to discover that back in January 1943, just before they had been interned, Britain and the USA had rescinded their rights awarded by the Unequal Treaties and had returned the treaty ports to China. While Shanghai was under Japanese occupation, it had been administered by Wang Ching-wei and his puppet regime, although Wang had been ill for the final war years and died of pneumonia on November 10th, 1944. Now it was a Chinese city and foreigners no longer had extra-territorial rights. It would take them some time to understand the full implications of this, but in the meantime everyone's priority was to get the city up and running again.

Although the members of the Shanghai Municipal Council were all Chinese from now on, they were very conscious that they still needed the expertise of the foreigners, and encouraged them to stay on in the city and revive their old businesses or to start new ones. Initially, their policy was to return foreign assets, both business and personal, to the original owners, especially those who had stayed loyal to Shanghai to the end, and had been interned. Shanghailanders were asked to register claims for the property that they had owned or occupied at the time of the Japanese takeover and, where this was feasible, their claims were recognized. Many people were able to return to what was left of their homes, but claiming business property, which was now under a different use or had been destroyed, was more complicated. They also had to deal with the corruption of Nationalist officials, who wasted no time in finding ways to extort bribes or confiscate desirable assets.

Eric immediately registered a claim for 108 Tifeng Road and was delighted when he received permission to return home. When he was strong enough, he went to look at the house, and was overwhelmed with emotion to discover that Cookie and his wife, our house amah, had already moved back in and were trying to clean up the mess left by the Japanese residents. My father had removed those things of real value from the house before he closed it down in 1941, and had given these to a Chinese friend for safe-keeping. Although the furniture was mostly still there, it was dirty and damaged and he realised that he could not bring his wife and family to the house the way it was. He was still too ill to leave the rehabilitation centre, so gave Cookie some money to have the property cleaned and painted and to dispose of the mattresses, soft furnishings and anything else that could be replaced.

❀   ❀   ❀   ❀   ❀

The months went by slowly. My father eventually recovered his health enough to leave the centre and move back home where Cookie and Amah could look after him. The house was full of ghosts and he longed to be united with his family. He was able to receive letters fairly regularly, so he knew that we were still in Canada, waiting for a ship to take us back to Britain. After all those years in the camp, I can understand his impatience to resume a normal family life and make up for those wasted years. He tried to find our baby amah, Ah Wong, but all he could discover was that she had returned to her village after we sailed to San Francisco, so was not in Shanghai for the Japanese occupation. We all hoped she was still alive and well. Our chauffeur had also disappeared. He had probably joined one of the armies but we never found out what became of him.

Time hung heavy on his hands, so after a while Eric decided to go back to work at the Shanghai Power Company for as many hours a week as he could manage. There was a whole new generation of Chinese engineers, trying to service the city with old, out-of-date equipment, so they were glad to have the old-timers back on the job as consultants. Power lines were destroyed or damaged all over the city. The municipalities of Chapei, Pootung and Yangtzepoo, where most of the factories had been located, were still in ruins and men like my father were invaluable for their knowledge and experience. Eric had been the vice president in charge of the industrial section at the Shanghai Power Company before the Japanese occupation, so he was reluctant to see other people take over his territory and being back on the job gave his life some focus.

He was finally given permission to leave and sailed from Shanghai on the *SS Strathmore* for Britain, arriving in Southampton, England on April 30th, 1946, eight months after being liberated from the Pootung Civilian Assembly Centre.

TOGETHER AGAIN

1946

I will never forget the day the Red Cross called us in White Rock to say that my father was alive and safe. We had just returned to school after the summer holidays, so it must have been in late September 1945. They gave us no details; only that he had been liberated and was in a rescue centre in Shanghai where he would be well looked after, fed and given medical aid. They also said that it would probably be some months before he could be sent home to Britain, and that our names had been put on a waiting list to be repatriated too when space in a ship became available. In the meantime, we were to continue our lives as normal until we heard more from them. We were enormously relieved and excited, but had so many unanswered questions. Eventually, after several weeks, we received a note from father saying that he was alright, getting stronger every day and waiting for a place on a ship. From then on, we were able to exchange letters from time to time. As it turned out, it was almost eight months before we would be all together again in Scotland.

We also heard that Mary, Ian and Maureen had returned to Scotland in March 1944, as Mary had developed a severe type of diabetes that could not be treated satisfactorily in India. Their ship was part of the first convoy to pass through the Suez Canal since it had been retaken by the Allied Forces. There were still many U-boats around and Ian remembers that they had to wear lifejackets all the time, even at night. Arriving safely in Liverpool, they were horrified at the severe bomb damage to both the port and the city. For the next three years, they lived with Mary's parents on a farm in Perthshire.

Just before that last Christmas in Canada, we had a cable to say that my grandmother, Elsie Duthie, had died on December 23rd, 1945. My mother was upset that she could not have waited just a few more months until we returned to Scotland. This meant that we had lost two grandparents since our last home leave. We finally received notice of our ship reservations to return to Britain. The eternal waiting was over. Our new friends gave many parties to say farewell to us, and we were filled with gratitude to them for all their kindness for almost five years. I knew that I would miss the Lee family especially. They had been my one link left to the China that I loved. We crossed Canada by train to Saint John, New Brunswick and sailed to Manchester, England on a ship called the *Manchester Port,* arriving on March 13th, 1946.

❀   ❀   ❀   ❀   ❀

Arriving back in Britain, we spent a few days in Edinburgh to look for a house to rent and to enrol Colin and me at George Watson's College for the summer term. We then went north to Sandhaven to spend Easter with my mother's family, the Duthies. Grandfather James Duthie was still very much in mourning for his wife, and I spent a lot of my time talking to him. He was a wonderful old man, tough as nails and enormously respected in the community. He was the master cabinet-maker at J & G Forbes Boat Builders, and also taught cabinet-making at the local trade school. Even at the age of 84, he still rode everywhere on his bicycle. He owned and lived in a two-storey stone house right across from the North Sea in Sandhaven and we took long walks together along the beach. One day I complained about the cold east wind blowing off the sea and he replied: "You're a Scot, laddie, so you'd better get used to it." This comment had a profound effect on me and it finally gave me a sense of my true identity.

I had always called myself a British Shanghailander, but re-alised that this meant nothing to people outside China, and I had been struggling with my identity. Before this, Scotland was a place that we visited from time to time on leave to see family, and Canada was just a temporary home while we waited for the war to end. Finally, I discovered that first and foremost I was a Scot: one with a Canadian accent and little knowledge of my real homeland, but this was something solid that no-one could take away from me. From then on, when people asked me what I was, I answered: "I'm a Scot, just like you." This was enor-mously important to me, especially when I went back to school, and it gave me a lot of new confidence.

Starting school again at Watson's was a frightening eye opener! I had been top of my class all the way through school in White Rock with very little effort, but now I found that I was two-and-a-half years behind other boys of my own age, and more in some subjects like Latin, which I had never taken. This was a very serious situation for me at 15 years of age if I want-ed to go on to University and a profession. Colin was also be-hind, but at 10 this was not so difficult and they dropped him a grade at the beginning of the year. George Watson's is a truly excellent school, with an interesting history going back to 1741, and was established as a college for boys in September 1871 by the Merchant Company of Edinburgh. The wonderful teachers said they would work with me after school to help me catch up slowly, if I took my studies seriously. I accepted the challenge, but it needed a tremendous effort on both their part and mine. Luckily, I was not the only boy from strange parts of the world returning after the war. Some of them had actually been in-terned with their families and were further behind than I was, so we worked together and formed some firm friendships.

※　※　※　※　※

We were officially informed that father was returning on the P. & O. *SS Strathmore*, arriving at Southampton on April 30th, 1946. We were also told that, under no circumstances, were we to go to the docks to meet him. He and the other passengers would be brought to London and they suggested that we chose one of the hotels on their list, give them the information, and wait there until he arrived at that address.

My mother booked us into the Marble Arch Hotel, which we had stayed at several times before on our way to or from Shanghai, so it was familiar to all of us. That was an awful day. We had no idea what time he would arrive, or even if he would arrive, and we spent the whole day waiting with a few other families in the lobby, growing more and more concerned. I finally fell asleep on a sofa and woke to hear the hall porter talking to my mother. Just behind him was a small man in badly fitting clothes and, to my astonishment, my mother leapt up and embraced him. Neither Colin nor I recognized him; he seemed diminished and emaciated with big eyes that were streaming with tears. He had never been a tall man, but had been strong and healthy when we last saw him. Now I was taller than he was, and probably weighed half as much again. I felt acutely embarrassed and did not know what to say. Eventually, big hugs all around solved that problem and the rest of the day passed somehow in a blur of mixed emotions.

The following day we relaxed, walked in Hyde Park and then, after dinner, took a taxi to King's Cross Station where we boarded the *Flying Scotsman* for an overnight trip back to Edinburgh and our new life together. Colin and I had missed a couple of days of school, so we immediately immersed ourselves back in our school work and sports.

The next few months were not easy. Our father seemed unable to accept the drab existence of post-war Britain. The country was full of badly dressed, demobilized servicemen looking for jobs or recovering from injuries and other traumas. The most basic of foods were still rationed, as were petrol, clothes and fabric, and everything not rationed seemed to be hard to get. He hated to see my mother wearing a house dress working in the kitchen without any help, and felt that I was spending so many hours at school just to avoid him. Of course this was not true, but there were times that I was grateful to be out of the house.

Colin managed better with Dad than I did. He had more time and seemed to be happy just to sit down and chat with him, perhaps because he was so much younger. I was almost 16, had been the man-of-the-house for five years and was finding it hard to adjust to having a father around. On top of this, I really did have a huge challenge to catch up with my school work. It was hard to know what to talk about, as so many subjects were taboo for a while. Later he opened up a bit about what he had been through, but not in those first few weeks.

Father's health slowly improved and he finally gained some weight. However, he tired easily, slept badly and had to eat small meals several times a day. It would be years before he could digest a normal meal in one sitting. He was endlessly restless and obviously frustrated with his own limitations and the restrictions imposed on him by circumstances outside his control. At times he argued with my mother over stupid little things, and I had to control my urge to come to her support. She was so patient with him that it almost broke my heart at times.

Years later, as a mature adult and as a medical practitioner, I understood that all this was perfectly normal, and that it was happening to millions of other families all around the world, but at the time it was hard to live with. Father was 46 years old and had a family to support. I think he was really frightened about how he would cope with the future. The Japanese had taken five really important years of his life. This had left him with poor health and he was totally out of step with the big advances in the science of electrical engineering that had taken place during and because of the war. He had every reason to be concerned.

⊛　⊛　⊛　⊛　⊛

Spring struggled against the bitter north winds and the damp of Edinburgh, and we all yearned for warm sunshine and the return of the spring flowers. Slowly, the weather improved and our spirits with it. When Colin and I finished the school year, my united family decided to take a holiday and explore the west coast of Scotland by car, stopping at inns along the way. Our friends had pooled their petrol coupons to help us do this and we were all excited. I celebrated my 16th birthday at Rothsay and this was the first truly happy day for all of us since my dad had come home. We felt like a real family again. The weather was soft and balmy and we found a lovely small seaside hotel in a rocky cove. Colin and I swam with the seals and we dined on fish and chips. I really fell in love with the west coast of Scotland on this holiday and returned frequently from then on.

When we got home to Edinburgh in mid-August, my mother told me that father had applied for transport to take him back to Shanghai. As an employee returning to an essential job, he was qualified to travel in returning troop carriers and even aircraft. She said that, eventually, she and Colin would join him, but would have to wait for reservations on a scheduled passenger ship, and this might not be for several months. I was to stay in school in Edinburgh and would go to live with my aunt Jean when they left. Although I was shocked at the news, I suppose I always knew that they would return to Shanghai. Father had even talked about that in his letters before he was repatriated, and his chances of finding a job in post-war Britain were slim. The house in Tifeng Road was freshly painted and Cookie and Amah were waiting. They were going home to Shanghai, but without me.

SORTING OUT OUR LIVES
1946 – 1947

I am not quite sure when or how my father returned to Shanghai, but it was some time that autumn. We came back from school one day and he was packing. The next day he left. Colin and I settled back into school life and, between extra catch-up classes and lots of sports, our days were totally filled. Mother seemed more relaxed and I imagine she went back to spending much of her time with her old friends. We chatted over dinner in the evenings, but otherwise seemed to have been absorbed in our own lives. As it turned out, it was not until the following March that my mother and Colin left for Shanghai too, so we were able to spend Christmas together. They sailed on the P. & O. *SS Strathmore* from Southampton on March 4th, 1947. Strangely, this was the same ship that had brought my father home to us the previous year.

I went to live with my Auntie Jean Colterjohn in her flat in Falcon Avenue, on the south side of Edinburgh and not far from Watson's. She was a large, rather plain woman but had a heart of gold and was very kind to me. She had a very demanding job working as a nurse for Professor Percival, a well-known dermatologist, so we quickly settled into a routine of helping each other when we could, but otherwise respecting the other's busy life. We mostly had breakfast and dinner together, but I was free to come and go as I pleased. I missed my family badly at first, but gradually filled the vacuum with other things.

George Watson's College was famous for its tight, but fair discipline and the very high standard of both its academics and sports, but academics always came first. It was a huge school, with several classes in each grade, streamed to different standards. Originally, I had been placed in the grade suitable for my age, but in a lower level. When it became apparent how much I had to catch up, and that I was hoping to go on to university, I was dropped a grade but raised to the top level. This worked well for me, and I continued to take as many catch-up classes as I could find time for, and this really paid off.

My social life mainly revolved around sports, with Boy Scouts and the occasional school dance as a diversion. I loved rugby and was captain of the first school team for two years. My best friend, Tom Yule and I were involved in the swimming and diving teams and competed in many intercity events, which we really enjoyed. I also joined the Officer Cadets and learned to shoot rifles. In fact, I was a member of the team that shot at the Bisley Gun Club several times. We stayed at the London Scottish Club and met boys from some of the famous English public schools. We thought them to be awful snobs, and were always delighted when we beat them in competitions. My life became full of interesting challenges, lots of sports, good friends and a caring Auntie Jean to look after me.

❀   ❀   ❀   ❀   ❀

We eventually heard that my father, Eric, had returned to Shanghai on a troop carrier: an old passenger ship that had been stripped down to bare essentials in order to hold as many people as possible. He shared a cabin, originally designed for two, with three other men. To start with they were courteous to each other but kept their stories to themselves. Eric was grateful to be on his way back to Shanghai and appreciated the time to come to grips with his life. Much as he loved us, his family, he had felt weak and useless for those months in Scotland. We had come from the war years in Canada, strong and healthy, sound in body and mind. Even in Edinburgh this had been conspicuous, and accentuated the differences in the way we had spent the last few years. To returning prisoners like my father, the gap was almost insurmountable.

We had tried so hard to understand and sympathise with what my father had been through, but it had been so bad that it was simply beyond our comprehension. The thing that hit him most forcibly was the way that we seemed to have managed so well without him. He could see no way that he was needed, and this made him feel inadequate and impotent. He had a beautiful wife in the prime of life and two wonderful children, but their lives had developed without him, and he was no longer part of them. We liked music foreign to his ears and talked enthusiastically about things of which he had never heard. He was desperately looking forward to returning to the familiar world of Tifeng Road and the loving attentions of Cookie and Amah. He knew returning to the Shanghai Power Company would be full of new challenges, but it was his world and he was still respected there.

As the trip progressed, the four men slowly let down their guard and discovered that they had much in common. By talking about what they had been through, they helped each other face up to their ghosts and, in effect, developed a therapy group. They drew strength from each other and my father soon learned that, bad as his experiences had been, others had fared worse. One man had been an RAF pilot and had been shot down over Germany, where he had been taken prisoner of war and had witnessed things from which he would never recover. His girlfriend had married someone else, and he could not stand the constant reminders of the war in Britain. He was on his way to a job on a tea estate in Ceylon.

The other two had been prisoners of the Japanese. One had been a rubber planter in Malaya, and had somehow ended up in Changi Jail in Singapore. He was returning to Malaya hoping to revive his rubber business. The fourth man had worked in Hong Kong and had left on a ship that had been torpedoed. He spent most of the war being moved from camp to camp on Sumatra and was now returning to Hong Kong. He had evacuated his family in time for them to reach England safely. However, they had been living in London and were all killed in a direct hit to their house in an air raid. He lost his mother, his wife and two children in this, so had no reason to want to stay in Britain. By the time they each reached their destination port, they were feeling stronger and more able to pick up the pieces of their lives and move on.

Eric realised that he was actually one of the lucky ones. All the members of his family were alive and well, and they still loved him. He was on his way back to his old house in the city in which he felt most at home, in spite of all the changes that the Japanese occupation had made. He knew that it was now up to him to get well, mentally and physically, so that he could welcome my mother and Colin when they arrived, and be the head of the family once more. It was many years later, and after I had married and had children of my own, that my father explained all this to me in one of his rare moments of confidence. I felt so proud of him. He was a survivor.

RETURN TO SHANGHAI

1946 – 1949

Immediately after the war, anti-Communist paranoia developed in many Western countries, especially in the USA, so it is understandable that American politicians felt that supporting Chiang Kai-shek was very important. Between 1945 and 1948, the United States poured about three billon US dollars into China. About a billion dollars of this was in food, medicine and essential supplies, and was made available through the United Nations Relief & Rehabilitation Administration (UNRRA). This saved an unimaginable number of lives and kick-started the recovery of the Chinese economy. Unfortunately, the Nationalist government insisted that this be distributed through their own agency, the Chinese National Relief & Rehabilitation Administration (CNRRA), and much of this aid got diverted to the black market or into the pockets of corrupt officials.

By the time Eric arrived back in Shanghai in the autumn of 1946, the city had shrugged off the horrors of the war years and the economy appeared to be booming. The department stores were full of luxury goods, still unavailable in Britain or Europe, and the restaurants served a variety of food and alcohol undreamed of elsewhere. The spirit of free trade, that had always been the life blood of Shanghai, appeared to be strong. However, it did not take him long to realise that things were not as healthy as first impressions had suggested. Inflation was rampant and the Chinese dollar was losing its value so fast that

people had to spend their earnings immediately, before it de-
valued further. Those foreigners who were paid in their own
national currency were able to enjoy the good life, but to the
Chinese this was devastating, and many had to turn to barter
as a means of survival.

Sam also returned to Shanghai and joined Eric there for a
while. He had left his job in India and had to decide what to do
with the rest of his life. He was 52 years old and still had a
family to support. The brothers' reunion was a great joy to
them both, especially being back in Shanghai again after all
those difficult years. There was no doubt in Eric's mind that
his immediate future was with the Shanghai Power Company.
He had been welcomed back warmly and was enjoying training
the new generation of Chinese engineers. He had to catch up
on all the advances in technology that had developed during
the war, but found this interesting. They had received new
equipment from the USA and his job was challenging and sat-
isfying. This was the therapy that Eric needed so badly.

However, Sam saw no future for himself in the new, and
now Chinese, city. General Electric was responding to the
changed environment enthusiastically, but hiring young Chinese engineers for its new plants. Sam said goodbye to Eric
and Shanghai and sailed back to Scotland, arriving in London
on December 12th, 1946.

My mother and Colin finally sailed from Southampton to
Shanghai in March, 1947. They arrived in early April, in a particularly beautiful spring, and I can only imagine the welcome
that my father, Cookie and Amah had waiting for them. My
mother indulged in a wonderful spending spree, filling the
house with new furnishings and making it a home again. Colin
went back to school, but the classes were very different from
the pre-war days. There were children from many countries,
with about two-thirds of the class Chinese. Many of these had
returned to Shanghai from spending the war years in America,
so were fluent in English and the ideals of Western culture.
Colin was well placed after a couple of terms at George Wat-

son's, which must have helped him get used to yet one more change of school.

⊛   ⊛   ⊛   ⊛   ⊛

As my family resumed their life in Tifeng Road, things were changing around them politically. Chiang Kai-shek had more or less kept the many different factions of China under his over-all control while they fought Japan as a common enemy. After eight years of war, everyone was exhausted, hungry and keen to get back to a normal life. The temptation of the American aid flowing into China was too great for many Nationalist officials, and corruption became wide-spread. The war with the Communists had resumed in earnest in July 1946, and this seems to have consumed all Chiang's energies. He was either finally unable to, or simply disinterested in, controlling other aspects of running the country from then on. Perhaps, he was burned out after all those years of fighting.

In 1943 in Cairo, Chiang had requested that all Chinese properties that had been confiscated by Japan after the first Sino-Japanese War, including Taiwan (Formosa) and the Penghu Islands (Pescadores), be returned to China, if the Japanese were defeated. In 1945, Japan surrendered these lands to China on behalf of the Allies under the terms of the Potsdam Declaration, but it was not until 1952 that the Japanese actually gave up sovereignty of these properties. When Japan had taken over Taiwan in 1895, they had eliminated most of the Aboriginal and Chinese residents, and it was now very much part of Japan. However, Chiang recognized that this would be a perfect retreat for the Republic of China and the Nationalist Government if they lost the war with the Communists. From 1946, Chiang began to move money and equipment to Taiwan to prepare for a possible evacuation from mainland China.

⊛   ⊛   ⊛   ⊛   ⊛

Soon after the Japanese surrendered, the Nationalist officials had started to persecute any Chinese who had remained in

Japanese-occupied China during the war, and somehow still possessed some wealth. They were labelled as collaborators, regardless of what they had suffered during the war years. In many cases their properties and bank accounts were confiscated, and those resisting were often executed. This resulted in a mass exodus of wealthy Chinese to other countries, especially America. Corrupt officials either stripped these businesses of their assets, or set them up in opposition to private enterprise. Protection rackets became common with violent threats to those businesses that would not pay. Eventually, many foreigners found trying to do business under this regime too difficult and gave up, returning to their home countries or moving to others like Malaya and Australia.

In other ways, the demographics of Shanghai were changing once again. In those post-war years, Shanghai had revolving doors; as some moved out, others moved in. The White Russian community of about 25,000 reduced in size by half between 1946 and 1948, as the Soviet Union offered Russians living abroad repatriation and citizenship. Thousands of Jews left to help build the new state of Israel. Hungry peasants flooded into the city at a rate that officials could not cope with, and many dropped dead in the streets, penniless and starving. Their land had been devastated by the war and they had hoped for help in the apparently affluent city.

If these reasons were not enough to discourage the citizens of Shanghai, the rampant inflation was often the final straw. Chiang Kai-shek reserved 80 per cent of his budget for the armed forces and his war with the Communists, leaving only 20 per cent to run the country. As this was insufficient, he printed new money whenever it was needed. By the middle of 1948, the exchange rate of the Chinese dollar to one U.S. dollar was a million to one. In a last attempt to save the situation, Chiang intervened in August and created a new gold Yuan pegged to the U.S. dollar at four to one. These cost three million old Chinese dollars each. Citizens were ordered to surrender all their gold, silver and foreign currency to the banks, to help stabilize the new Yuan, but even this was useless. The government made no changes to their spending habits and the gold Yuan started to slip within a month. All this achieved was to alienate the remaining loyal middle classes, who had given up their gold and savings for nothing.

⊛   ⊛   ⊛   ⊛   ⊛

As the autumn of 1948 approached, my parents and many of their friends started to re-evaluate their future in Shanghai seriously. The Chinese economy had collapsed and rumours of Communist victories were starting to get through to Shanghai, in spite of the strict control of the press. Eric had become aware that he was no longer really needed at the Shanghai Power Company, as younger and technically superior Chinese engineers were able to do a better job than he was. He was also having health problems, as a result of years of starvation during the war. It was still an American-controlled private company and, after some discussion, they agreed that Eric should retire at the end of the year with a full pension. He was only 49 years old in December of that year, but his useful life with the Company was finished.

My parents, Eric and Amy, packed up our home in Tifeng Road and shipped their personal things back to Scotland. They must have felt ambivalent as they did this. Shanghai was no longer the carefree, fun-loving treaty port of the 1920s and 1930s, but they had invested the best years of their lives there, and it must have been hard for them to face the realities of what Shanghai had become. Sometime in December, or possibly in early January 1949, they said a sad farewell to Cookie and Amah and their remaining Shanghai friends, and flew to Australia. They knew many Shanghailanders who had retired there, and thought they should explore Australia and New Zealand before returning to Scotland. Poor Colin had to leave his familiar surroundings once again.

⊛   ⊛   ⊛   ⊛   ⊛

From the middle of 1948, the Communists made significant progress and captured many of the northern cities that were still garrisoned by the Nationalist armies. One by one, Nationalist generals chose to surrender, rather than to continue the siege with starvation and probable death, and defected to the Communist People's Liberation Army (PLA). They brought with them enormous amounts of arms and equipment, much of it from U.S. aid. In December, they captured Suchow on the Grand Canal. This was a defining blow to the Nationalists, and Chiang started preparations to move the government to Taiwan. On January 21st, 1949 Chiang Kai-shek formally resigned, handing over control of the Nationalist government to Li Tsung-jen. In reality, Chiang continued to control much of the armed forces and those government officials close to him, which made Li's position impossible.

In February, the gold and silver reserves were spirited out of the Bank of China in Shanghai in the middle of the night and shipped to Taiwan. Nationalist officials, loyal to Chiang, and senior officers in the armed forces followed, moving their families and wealth there too. As the PLA reached the north shore of the Yangtze River, Chiang ordered his prime troops to withdraw and to refuse to fight, eventually sending them to Taiwan. The army that was left made a token stand, but many units defected to the PLA as it advanced. They built up a huge force along the north bank of the river and commandeered every boat they could find of any size. In the evening of April 21st, this flotilla of thousands of small boats crossed the Yangtze, with only light resistance, and took over the south shore. Nanking was taken without a fight.

Things in Shanghai were in chaos by this time. Martial law had been declared, corruption and inflation had destroyed the economy, and the press was muzzled. Rumours of the impending arrival of the Communists brought hope that they would be able to return some law and order to the city where everyone else had failed. The city fathers sent envoys to meet Mao Tse-tung's leaders and negotiated a peaceful takeover of Shanghai.

Late on May 24th and early on May 25th, 1949 the Communists marched into Shanghai and quietly took over the city.

Meanwhile, Chiang Kai-shek, his loyal forces, government officials and their families were starting a new life in Taiwan with much of China's gold and silver reserves to ease their way. Opinion has always been divided on whether this was an act of heroism or treachery. By doing what he did, he rescued enough of the Nationalist resources to be prepared to make another stand against the Communists in the future, if they failed in their attempt to run the country successfully. On the other hand, there were those who felt that, if he had fought to keep the Communists north of the Yangtze, he might have held at least half the country in Nationalist control. Perhaps Chiang was simply worn out after trying to hold China together through eight years of war against the Japanese and four years of fighting the Communists, and there was no-one strong enough to take his place. Chiang Kai-shek finally died in Taiwan on April 5th, 1975. The rest is history.

EDINBURGH

1949 – 1955

In the spring of 1949, I had to decide whether to continue at Watson's for another year or to leave early and apply to the medical school at Edinburgh University. I was already behind for my age, and keen to get on with my life. Luckily, George Watson's College had a wonderful head master at that time, Mr. Andrews. Initially, he tried to persuade me to stay on, but he eventually agreed that I was ready for university. He had supported me through all those difficult years since I had returned from Canada, and now he called the dean of medicine, explained my situation, and made me an appointment for an interview. Apparently I did well, as I was accepted for enrolment in September, subject to receiving good marks in my final examinations. I owe Mr. Andrews and Watson's my deepest gratitude for the way they moulded and supported my ambitions though those important years. And so I was ready to move on to the next phase of my life, excited and well prepared.

❇ ❇ ❇ ❇ ❇

Just before Easter, on March 24th, 1949, my family arrived back from Australia, and Colin returned to Watson's for the third time. They had decided that Australia and New Zealand were not for them, so had cut their trip short. They felt these countries were for young people and they were too old to make the adjustment. Scotland was to be their home from now on. They rented a house not far from our school and started their new life. I was rather reluctant to leave my Aunt Jean, as I had grown very fond of her and had enjoyed a lot of freedom there, but understood that I needed to get to know my family again. Colin had missed a term of school while they were travelling and found the classes really hard. I coached him whenever I had time, but all these school changes had taken their toll and he was not as motivated as I had been to catch up. However, he quickly found a place on the rugby team and excelled at other sports too, which at least boosted his confidence.

That was my last term at school and it flew past. I graduated with high marks in almost all subjects and was really excited about going on to university in the autumn. I found a few odd jobs over the summer holidays, like cutting other people's lawns and pumping petrol, but mostly I just enjoyed doing things with my family. We had another trip to the west coast and lots of day excursions. I even learned to play golf with my father.

❋   ❋   ❋   ❋   ❋

I fell in love with Edinburgh University that very first day. A senior professor welcomed the new class with the following: "Ladies and gentlemen, one of God's greatest gifts to mankind is the ability to learn, and you have the privilege of learning at one of the world's oldest and greatest universities. From now on, your days will be filled with learning, and this will not stop when you leave your classes. You will keep learning as you walk around this ancient city, browse the book-stalls and drink in the pubs. You will learn from your teachers and you will learn from one-another. Do not only read your prescribed textbooks. Above all, read history and learn from those who went before you. One day, you may even have the privilege of teaching what you have learned to those who come after you." I have never forgotten his words.

I left that lecture hall exhilarated in a way I had never felt before. I knew absolutely that I was in the right place at the right time. There were so many wonderful things to choose from that I hardly knew where to start, but we were advised to enroll for the classes that we wanted to attend, before all the places were taken. After that, there were dozens of clubs, academic and sporting, that we could sign up for, and I could not believe that there would be enough hours in each day for all the things I wanted to do. I enrolled for rugby and swimming at once, but left other choices for later. I still had to scramble around the bookstores to find the textbooks I needed for the best prices, and the competition was fierce. It all became a bit of a game, with second-year students holding back the hardest-to-find books, and then selling them to us for higher prices when we got desperate. By lunchtime, we were so exhausted we collapsed into the nearest pub for mutton pies and a beer. That was also the day that new friendships started. Gerry, Charlie, David, Bob and Mike were there and we would all stay together and support each other for the next six years.

❀ ❀ ❀ ❀ ❀

By now, I had been living in Edinburgh for several years but my life had revolved around Watson's, the various rugby pitches and swimming pools where I had played, and the area around my Aunt Jean's home. I was now free to roam the streets of Edinburgh, take short cuts through the wynds and closes, and sit with my friends in the ancient pubs of the Old Town. I browsed in the secondhand bookshops close to the university, and was thrilled to discover an early edition of Adam Smith's *The Wealth of Nations* and several gems by Sir Walter Scott.

When I needed some fresh air and exercise, I climbed the Carlton Hill or Arthur's Seat with my friends. Occasionally, I would stroll down Leith Walk to Portobello and the Port of Leith and look at the ships. I knew that my great-grandfather, Wilhelm Colterjahn, had arrived there from Germany and wondered about him. Slowly, I became part of Edinburgh and it reached deep into my soul. I had lost my much-loved Shanghai, but realized that Edinburgh was taking its place. I had generations of family roots here, and that made me feel that I truly belonged.

Edinburgh is sometimes called the *Athens of the North*, because of its beautiful, neo-classic architecture and the fact that it is built on seven hills. However, it does not have Greece's climate. Winter is cold and grey with a thick *haar* (fog) lying low over the city. In the 1950s, this trapped in the noxious coal smoke from thousands of chimneys, painting everything from the buildings to one's clothes black; hence Edinburgh's nick name of *Auld Reekie* (Old Smokey). Eventually, the city fathers outlawed coal fires, and today the buildings are cleaner and the atmosphere much improved. However, even in the summer, the bitter winds off the North Sea can chill one to the bone. When the sun does shine and there is no wind or rain, it is the most beautiful city on earth.

❀   ❀   ❀   ❀   ❀

The weeks rolled into months and it seemed no time before I was graduating from my first year at medical school. I spent the summer working as a ward orderly at Ballochmyle Hospital, near Mauchline in East Ayrshire. I was at the bottom of the hospital pecking order, but it was an excellent way to get used to hospital routines and protocol. I enjoyed it so much that I signed up for the following summer before I left.

My parents spent this time looking for a permanent home to buy. They chose a house called Grange Neuk in the village of West Linton, about 20 miles south of Edinburgh. It was right on the highway - the last house on the left going south out of town. It was a pretty house, surrounded by a big garden, and had a lovely view looking down over the River Lyne and the village green. They took possession of this in August 1950, so from then on, Colin and I had half an hour's bus trip to school. We all liked West Linton and gradually made friends there. My parents played a lot of bridge and spent many hours working in the garden. There was a friendly golf club and I enjoyed playing with my father at weekends. The Colterjohn family really seemed to be settling down at last.

The following year, in October 1951, I met the girl who would become my wife one day, Elizabeth Shaen Orr, better known as Libby. She lived with her family in a big old house on a country property called Spittlehaugh, about a mile and a half outside West Linton. Her father was a prominent Edinburgh solicitor. She was taking a year off between school and training to be an occupational therapist, and had just returned from a few months in Canada. She was bubbling over with a love of life and had all the things a young man looks for in a girl. I immediately fell under her spell. We became good friends at once, but we both realized there were many years to go before I would graduate as a doctor.

For the next two summers, I worked as a loader and driver at a huge commercial shooting lodge in the highlands. They catered to the rich and famous from all over the world, who came there to shoot grouse. Luckily, I received such large tips that I was able to buy Libby an engagement ring. By this time, all my friends had steady girlfriends and our Saturday evenings were usually spent together at university dances. I was doing well in my courses, enjoying the practical hospital work, and had a wonderful girl who I loved. Life was good!

⚘   ⚘   ⚘   ⚘   ⚘

Uncle Sam and his family had decided to go to Canada, and we all missed them after they sailed for Montreal in the summer of 1949. Bill, the eldest of the three Colterjohn brothers, was the chief civilian accountant at the Royal Canadian Air Force base in Trenton, Ontario and he and his wife, Helen, provided Sam's family with a home for the first few months. Sam soon found an engineering job with the Central Bridge Company there.

Ian worked for a while and then joined the RCAF, receiving his wings and a commission in 1951. Sadly, he was diagnosed with Grave's Disease and spent a year in hospital in Winnipeg. This was the end of his air force career, but he met and fell in love with one of the nurses, Marjorie Ayers. They were married in 1953 and moved to Vancouver where Ian found a job with the British American Oil Company.

Maureen trained as a nurse at Queen's University, where she met her future husband, LeRoy Hall who was studying medicine there. They married in 1957 and moved to Picton, Ontario.

❋   ❋   ❋   ❋   ❋

1955 marked one hundred years since Wilhelm Colterjahn had landed in Leith and made it his new home. It also turned out to be a year full of endings and new beginnings. Libby graduated as an occupational therapist at Easter and took a job at Bridge of Earn Hospital and Rehabilitation Centre near Perth. I graduated as a doctor in June and started my first internship at the Edinburgh Royal Infirmary. Colin finished school at Watsons and took the summer off before starting an apprenticeship with a local farm equipment company.

My parents became restless and sold Grange Neuk. They found the winters in West Linton cold and rented a house in Kirn near Rothsay, hoping that the west coast climate would be warmer. As it happened, my father developed acute joint pains and was diagnosed with advanced osteoporosis from all those years of malnutrition. They returned to West Linton to be closer to hospitals and bought another house there called Linton Grange, at the north end of the village.

Sadly, my Aunt Jean died on September 26th from cancer of the caecum. She had been a good friend to me and I missed her very much. However, life goes on and Ian and Marjorie brought the first of a new generation into the world with the birth of Karen Jean.

Finally, Libby and I got married on December 2nd, 1955 to round off a very eventful year. But that is another story...

EPILOGUE

The Cold War against Communism had already started even before Germany and Japan were defeated by the Allies. Britain and the United States of America knew the biggest challenge would be Stalin and Russia, but hungry and oppressed people everywhere responded to the ideals of Communism. All over the Far East, South-east Asia and India, countries were surging towards independence from imperialism, and the Communists played a big part in fostering discontent and organizing riots. Not only was the mighty British Empire starting to collapse; the Dutch colonies in Indonesia, French Indochina and the American protectorates in the Pacific were straining at the leash.

The first to go was India. In August 1947, the jewel in the crown of the British Empire became two independent countries, India and Pakistan, although they remained associated with Britain as members of the Commonwealth of Nations. In the jungles of Malaya, the Chinese Communists, who had fought so bravely side-by-side with the British army guerrillas, had stolen supplies, equipment and arms dropped by the liberating U.S. Air Force. They had stashed them in the jungle for the future struggle against imperialism, and started guerilla attacks soon after the war ended. The British declared a state of emergency in Malaya which took twelve years to resolve.

One by one, the countries of the Far East and Southeast Asia fought for and won their independence, with many of them succumbing to Communism. As the Russians closed Eastern Europe behind the Iron Curtain, and the Chinese Communists took over China, the world became embroiled in conflict once again.

There was, and still is, no peace.

BIBLIOGRAPHY

I wish to thank the authors of the following books for help-ing me understand the background to my story in an era long gone. Although these are only a few of the books I used in my research, they are the ones that I would like to rec-ommend to anyone who enjoyed SHANGHAI Loved and Lost, and is looking for further reading on this subject.

CHINA:
SHANGHAI: The Rise And Fall Of A Decadent City - by Stella Dong (2000)
Empire of The Sun - by J. G. Ballard (1984)
Shanghai Girls - by Lisa See (2009)
The House of Exile - by Nora Waln (1933)
Wild Swans - by Jung Chang
The Long March - by Harrison E. Salisbury (1985)
The Fall of Shanghai - by Noel Barber
Tracing it Home - by Lynn Pan (1992) - she wrote several other books on China.
The Rape of Nanking - by Iris Chang (1997)
Forgotton Ally - by Rana Mitter (2013)
Captives of Empire: Japanese Internment of Allied Civilians in China 1941-1945 - by Greg Leck (2006- ISBN 0-9772141-0-9)

BURMA:
The Railway Man - by Eric Lomax (2009)
Elephant Company - by Vicki Croke (2014)

JAPAN:
A Boy Called "H" - by Kappa Senoh (1997)

SCOTLAND:
How The Scots Invented The Modern World - Arthur Herman (2001)

COLTERJAHN / COLTERJOHN FAMILY TREE

Martin Ferdinand Wilhelm Colterjahn m **Johanna Catherina Maria Thiems**
Born: Germany 1828   Born: Germany 1829
Died: Scotland 1899   Died: Scotland after 1900

Bertha 1857 - 1935
m. August Schlossmann d 1919
(1 son & 5 daughters)

Dorothea Henrietta 1859 - 1886
m. Gilbert Archer Jamieson
(no children)

Wilhelm Herrmann Colterjahn
1860 – 1889
(never married)

Albert Colterjahn 1862 - 1939
m. Catherine M. Duncan 1862 – 1919

Wilhelm (Bill) Colterjohn 1891 - 1979
m. Helen Anderson (in Canada)
(no children)

Jean McNicoll Colterjohn
1892 – 1955
(never married)

Samuel John Duncan Colterjohn
1994 – 1978
m. Mary Jacks Tait 1907 – 1965

Albert Eric Colterjohn 1899 - 1973
m. Emily(Amy) Duthie 1905 - 1993

Sam & Mary

Eric & Amy

Albert Ian Colterjohn 1931 -
m. Marjorie Ayers 1953 –
(1 son & 2 daughters)

Janet Maureen 1936
m. Le Roy Hall
(3 sons & 1 daughter)

Eric Duncan Colterjohn 1930 – 2005
m. Elizabeth Shaen Orr 1933 -
(3 sons & 1 daughter)

Colin Duthie Colterjohn
1935 - 1957
(never married)

CHINA: TIMELINE OF HISTORICAL EVENTS

1842	August 29 - **TREATY OF NANKING** - making 5 international treaty ports and Hong Kong a British colony.
1843	first British merchants arrived in Shanghai.
1848	foreign population exceeded 100. Biggest British and U.S. trading companies moved from Canton to Shanghai.
1851-64	Civil War: **TAIPING REBELLION**
1860	Chinese Emperor died.
1860	**TREATY OF TIENTSING** ended Second Opium war.
	Foreign forces attacked and burned Peking Summer Palace.
	Foreigners became legally free to travel anywhere in China and 4 new Treaty ports were created inland.
	By taxing opium, Chinese effectively legalized opium.
	Advent of steam navigation along inland waterways - faster and larger cargos.
1861-1865	**American Civil War** cut off cotton exports to Britain. China benefited.
1863	The Shanghai Municipal Council created to administer International Settlement.
	French Concession became a municipality administered by the French Consul.
	2 foreign enclaves expanded to 3 times their original sizes and the port was now the sixth largest in the world.
1882	First power company was built. 1993 - it was bought by SMC.

1898-1900   **BOXER REBELLION** against foreigners. Chinese attacked foreign legations in Peking. Subdued by foreign armies but many foreigners killed.

Shanghai got the country's first modern printing press and publishing industry.

Young educated Chinese elite moved to Shanghai to wage war in words.

95% of the residents in the International Settlement were Chinese. They paid equal taxes with the foreigners but did not have equal rights.

1902   Formation of Chinese Chamber of Commerce in Shanghai.

1894   China lost war with Japan over Korea - **TREATY OF SHIMONOSEKI**.

Penalties: Cession of Formosa & Pescadores to Japan. Korean independence.

Japan received Unequal Treaty privileges to 7 Chinese ports with industrial rights.

1905   Boycott of everything American. Started in Shanghai and spread to other cities.

Chinese demanded representation on the Municipal Council and was rejected.

1895 - 1910 Population of Shanghai doubled.

1911   **REVOLUTION**: The Wuchang Uprising overthrew the Ch'ing Dynasty. Empress Dowager and the boy emperor sent into exile. China became a republic.

1912   Dr. Sun Yat-Sen became provisional president of the Republic of China.

1910 - 1930 Population tripled to almost 3,000,000

1915   Japan became the foreign country with the most nationals in Shanghai.

1916 - 1926 **Warlord Era** - Political instability, both Nationally and in the cities.

1918   Opium banned. Great increase in all kinds of crime. Rise of gangster control.

1919   **Treaty of Versailles** gave leased lands confiscated from Germans to Japanese.

White Russians flooded Shanghai after Bolshevik war. No Extraterritoriality.

China asks USA, Britain and Germany for help, but they all turned China down.

1921   **Birth of the Chinese Communist Party**.   They started to organize strikes.

1923   Communists joined KMT in united front to unify the country and oust warlords.

Soviet Russia pledged aid to Sun Yat-Sen. Chiang Kai-Shek went to Moscow.

1924   Whampoa Military Academy opened with Russian help.

1920s   Shanghai jazz capital. 300 cabarets, night clubs & dance halls. U.S. movies very popular. Start of Chinese film industry.

1923   SMC cleaned up crime in International settlement. Many gangster bases moved to French concession. 3 separate jurisdictions made control almost impossible.

1925   **May 30th. Uprising**. General strike in Shanghai. 3,000 demonstrated against foreign privilege - Japanese & Westerners terrified. Spread to 28 other cities.

Communist Party grew to about 10,000 in Shanghai.

1925   March - **Sun Yat-Sen died**. Nationalists fought each other for control of KMT.

KMT proclaimed itself Nationalist government of China. Party split in 1926.

1926   Chiang Kai Shek took over as commander-in-chief of Nationalist army and launched Northern Expedition to fight Warlords. Communists Co-operated.

1927   Nationalist Revolutionary coalition Army captured Hankow, Kiukiang and Nanking and took back foreign concessions. 70,000 foreigners panicked in Shanghai.

1927   **21 March - Communists organized massive general strike** against Warlord rule.

1927   Foreign community bribed Kiang Kai Shek to break his alliance with the Reds and form an **Unholy Trinity** of Kuomintang, foreigners and the Green Gang.

Shanghai provisional Court created with Chinese magistrates to try Chinese cases.

1927   **April 12 - Massacre of Shanghai**. Kiang started the purge of the Communists.

New Nationalist HQ in Nanking.

All Russian Communist advisers were expelled.

Reign of terror - Chiang used extortion, kidnapping, blackmail and intimidation.

1927   December - Chiang married Soong Mei-ling. Divided party factions united.

1929   June - Nanking confirmed as the official home of the Nationalist Kuomintang Government with Chiang as leader. Recognized by the Western Powers.

1930s   Increase in Japanese aggression.

1931   Mukden Incident: Japan invaded Manchuria.

Japan established puppet state of Manchukuo.

1932   **January - Shanghai Incident:** Japan assault on Chinese areas of Shanghai.

1934/1936   Communist "Long March". 6,000 miles ending in North Shaanxi.

1936   December - Xian Incident: Chiang Kai-Chek was kidnapped by friendly warlords.

KMT and communists formed united front to fight Japanese.

1937   July - Marco Polo Bridge incident. **Official start of the Sino-Japanese war.**

Nationalist Government evacuated Nanking

1937   August 13 to November **- Fall of Shanghai to the Japanese**

1937   Dec. 13 - **Rape of Nanking**: over 300,000 killed

1938   20,000 Jews started to arrive in Shanghai from Nazi Europe

1939   **September 1 - WW2 in Europe**

1940   Most British troops left for Singapore and other strategic points.

June 10 - Italy joined Germany in the war.

June 22	France capitulated: signed armistice with Germany. French Concession administered by Vichy Government.
	September 27 - Germany, Italy and Japan signed Tripartite Pact (Axis Alliance)
1941	**December 7/8 - Japan attacked Pearl Harbor** and other Asian targets.
	Japanese took over of foreign concessions in Shanghai.
	December 8 - US & Britain **declared war on Japan.**
1943	February - **US and Britain relinquished their extraterritorial rights** and all Treaty Ports were returned to the Chinese, still under Japanese occupation.
1945	**May 8 - VE Day:** Germany surrendered
	August 14 - VJ Day: Japanese surrendered.
1946	Full scale war resumed between the KMT and communists.
1949	May 24 - Shanghai fell to Peoples Liberation Army.
1949	**October 1 - Mao Tse-Tung formally proclaimed the People's Republic of China.**

Timeline: World Events
1750 - 1914

1750 - 1850	Industrial Revolution in Britain
1757	Robert Clive conquered India
1759	James Wolfe captured Heights of Abraham in Quebec
1775 - 1783	American Revolution War of Independence
1789 - 1799	French Revolution (debatable end date)
1799 - 1815	British defeated Tipu Sultan's French army at Seringapatam, Mysore
1799 - 1815	Napoleonic Wars
1815 June	**Battle of Waterloo**
1807	Abolition of the slave trade by British parliament
1818	Agreement between Britain, Spain and Portugal to abolish slaves
1820s	Steamships started to come into general use
1821	Hudson Bay Company controlled over 3 million sq. miles of land in North America
1834	Morse code invented
1842	**Treaty of Nanking:** First British Treaty Ports in China
1848	Gold rush to California

1853-56	Dr. David Livingstone discovered Victoria Falls & crossed Africa
1857	Indian Mutiny (too many changes too fast)
Mid 1800s	Tea became a major export from India
1861-1865	**American Civil War**
1865	Emancipation of slaves in USA
1865	Telegraph wires from East to West across USA
1867	**British American Act created Canada**
1867	British stopped sending convict ships to Australia
1876	Graham Alexander Bell invented the telephone
1883	**Sir Sandford Fleming synchronized clocks around the world**
1885	CP railway completed in Canada from coast to coast
1905	Russian Revolution
1910	Mexican Revolution
1911	Chinese Revolution. Republic of China formed
1914-1918	**The Great War**

AUTHOR

ELIZABETH SHAEN COLTERJOHN was born and raised in Scotland. She and her husband, Duncan, spent several years living and working in England, Malaya and Zambia before immigrating to Ontario, Canada in 1967 with their four children and a Labrador. After they retired, the Colterjohns moved to the Lake Chapala area of Mexico, where Elizabeth is still living and writing.

The author can be contacted at elizabeth.shaen@gmail.com.

Printed in Great Britain
by Amazon.co.uk, Ltd.,
Marston Gate.